CORRUPTION IN PUBLIC SERVICES

Corruption in Public Services

Dr. N.K. Dutta

ANMOL PUBLICATIONS PVT. LTD.
NEW DELHI - 110 002 (INDIA)

ANMOL PUBLICATIONS PVT. LTD.
H.O.: 4374/4B, Ansari Road, Darya Ganj,
New Delhi-110 002 (India)
Ph.: 23278000, 23261597

B.O.: No. 1015, Ist Main Road, BSK IIIrd Stage
IIIrd Phase, IIIrd Block,
Bangalore - 560 085 (India)
Visit us at: www.anmolpublications.com

Corruption in Public Services

First Published, 2006

ISBN 81-261-2868-2

PRINTED IN INDIA

Printed at Mehra Offset Press, Delhi.

Dedicated to my Father
Late Sonaram Dutta
And My Mother
Srimati Sundari Dutta

Contents

Preface

Corruption in public services prevalent from the past become a burning problem in all the countries of the world. The objective of the work is to assemble a wide range areas polluted with corruption and the people working and corruption in developing countries with special reference to India, in order to take a comparative view of the phenomena and to bring together people with common interest who had so far not been in touch. The work is based on a vivid study of this burning issue with which the public servants are so entangled, prevalence of corruption never fails to evoke a gushing torrent of abuse, even from the most docile. This canker is fast destroying our economy and our morals. So, I feel it is high time to analyse the problem of corruption in respect of its causation and cures and expose their inadequacies. This public calamity is mighty leveller. There are occasions when any, even the slightest chance of doing good, must inconsiderable person.

The need to central this severe form of criminality is imperative. Although the adverse effects of this type of socio-economic offence is in evidence all around us and their far reaching consequences are obvious even to the common man sincere effort are yet to be given by the government as well as by the society itself to control and prevention in our country. The problem or corruption is very complex since it has its roots and ramifications in society as a whole. Corruption includes improper or selfish exercise of power and influence attached to a public office due to the special position one occupies in public life. So the problem is to be viewed in relation to the entire system or moral values and the socio-economic structure of society,

The Prevention of Corruption Act, 1947 was passed to make more effective provisions for the prevention of bribery and corruption as the existing law i.e. IPC was found insufficient to eradicate bribery and corruption from amongst the public servant. The PCA 1947 was later on amended twice once by the Criminal Amendment Act, 1952 and later in 1964 by the Santhanam Committee which was finally repealed Prevention of Corruption Act, 1988 to fill up the inadequacies of the 1947 Act.

The usefulness of the book to all concerned is beyond doubt. The book can be in equal measure be useful to the students of Criminal Law in the course of higher legal studies. The author discharge his obligation with sincere gratitude to all these who inspired to write this book.

Lastly I would be failing in my duty, if I do not place on record my thanks to my wife Dr Leena Dutta Bharali and my sons Mrinabh and Tarunabh for the sacrifices made by them during the period of my work and but for whose cooperation it would not have been completed.

—Dr. Nalini Kanta Dutta

Tables of Cases

Akhowri Inderdeo Prasad - V - State,
A.I.R. 1958, Pat. 374

Amarendra Nath Roy -V - State,
A.I.R 1955, Cal. 236

Amrit Lal - V - State of Punjab,
A.I.R. 1973, Cr.L.E. 210, 1973 Cur.I.J. 260

A. Verraili -V- State, A.I.R. 1975,
A.P. 663

A. Mohammed Pagarker-V - State (Union Territory of Goa), A I.R. 1960, S.C. 499, 1980 Cr.L.J. 220

Balakrishna -v- state of Orissa, 1971
Cr.L.J. 670(SC)

Balgopal Goenka -V- State of W.B., ., A.I.R.
1988, Cr.L.J. 570 (cal.)

Balaji -V- I.T.O., 1962, 2 SCR 983

Bal Krishna Sayal -V- State of Punjab (1987)
S.C. 689 (From Punjab and Haryana)

Banwari—V- State of Rajasthan, 1979,
Cr.L.J. 161 (Raj.)

Banshilal -V- State of Bihar
A.I.R. 1981, S.C. 1235, 1981 Cr.L.J. 741

Bas-Ul-Huq -V- State of W.B., A.I.R. 1953, S.C. 298,
S.C.R. 836,1953, Cr.L. 1232, 1953, S.C.J. 406

Bhagat Ram -V- State of Rajasthan, A.I.R 1972,
S.C, 1502 ,(1972)2 S.C .A. 38, 1972 S.C. Cr.R. 521

Ganga Narain -V- State, A.I.R-. 1966, All. 197

G.V. Nanjudiah V- State (Delhi: Administration, A.I.R:. 1967, G.C. 2402, 1998 Cr.L.J. 152, (1987) 3

Crimes 217, (1967)33 D.L.T. 96,1987 G.C. CR. R. 303 - (1987)3 serv. L.J. 244, 1987 Cr.L.R. (S.S.) 580, (1987)2 Sup. 345, (1987) Cal. Cr.L.R. (S.C.) 189, (1987) All.Cr.C. 450, (1987)3 I.J Rep. 589(1987)4 J.T. 313, (1987)23 Tex Law Rev. 1

Ginduchi patnaik -V- State of Orissa, A.I.R. 1985, Cr.L.J. 645 (Orissa)

Gokulchand Dawarkdas Morarka -V- The King, A.I.R. 1948, P.C. 82

Haradhan Char -v- State of W.B., A.I.R 1981, Cr.L.J. NOC 158 (Cal.)

Hari Dev Sharma -V- State, A.I.R. 1976, G.C. 1489 (1976)1 Serv. I.C. 246, 1976 Cr. App. R. (S.C.) 201, 1976 L.J. (S.C.) 802, 1976 Cr.L.J. 1176, 1976 CP.L.R. (S.C .) 246, (1976)2 S.C.W.R. 28, Overruling 1971, Cr.L.J 1615 (Delhi)

Hemanta Kumar Mohanty -V- State of Orissa, 1973(1) S.L.R. 112, 1973 (Cut.L.T.) 361

Hussainara Khatoon -V- State of Bihar, 1979 Cr.L.J. 1036 (S.C.) 1979, Cr. L.J. 1052 (S.C.) 65

H.T. Huntley-V- Emperor (1944), A.I.R., F.C.

45 Cr.L.J. 755, 214 I.C. 199, 1944 FLJ 17, 28 Pat. 517

Jai Ram Lakhe -V- State of Punjab, 1978 3 S.C.C. 133, 1978 Cr.L.R. 160, 1978 U.J. (S.C.) 266, (1978) 2 S.C.W.R. 104.1978 S.C.C (Cr.) 337, 1978 S.C. Cr.R. 235

Jai Narain -V- State, A.I.R. 1974, S.C. 228, (1974) 3 S.C.C. 598

Jaswant Singh -V- State of Punjab, A.I.R. 1973, S.C. 707,1973

Jogeswar Singh Rastogi -V- State of M.P A.I.R. 1980, S.C. 366(2), 1979 Cr.App. R. (S.C) 302 1980 Cr.L.J. 323

Kailash Chandra Babu -V- State of Orissa, 1988 (2) Orissa 609

Kanchan Singh Dholak Singh Thakur -V- State of Gujarat, A.I.R. 1979, S.C. 1011(2 Judges), (1979)4 S.C.C. 599, 1979 Vad. L.J. (Cr) 589, (1979) S.C.J. 260, (1379) U.J. (S.C.) 551,1979 Cur. L.J. (Cr.) 216, 1973 Cr.L.J. 889, 1976 Cr.L.R. (S.C.) 246

Khombu Ram -V- State, 1972 -Cr.L.J. 381 (Him. Pra), 1971 Sim. L.J (H.P.) 289

K.P. Sinha -V- Aftabuddin, A.I.R. 1955, Pat.453 84, 174 Kunhi Mohammed -V- State, A.I.R 1959, Kerala 88

Krishan Lal. -V- State, 1971, Cr.L.J. 1610 (Delhi)

Lalchand Topindas -V- State, A.I.R 1956. Orissa 201, I.L.R. 1366, Cut.517, 22 Cut.L.T. 397, 1936 Cr.J. 341

Loknath Dash -B- State of Orissa, 1977 Cr.L.J. 1268, 1977 Cut.L.R.(Cr.88) (1977) 43 Cut.L.T. 478 (Cri)(S.I.)

Makhan Lal -V- State, A.I.R. 1959, Rajasthan 214

Madan Mohan Singh -V- State of U.P., A.I.R. 1959, S.C. 637, 1954

Mohanlal Keshaval -V- State, A.I.R. 1966, Bombay 504

Matajong Dobey -V- H.C. Bhari, A.I.R. 1956, S.C. 44

Mehar Singh Hajra Singh -V- State (1955) Cr.L.J. 1887, A.I.R. 1955, Pepsu 156

Mitra -V- State, A.I.R. 1951, Cal.524

Moba Singh -V- State (Delhi Administration), A.I.R. 1976, S.C. 449,1976, Cr.L.J. 346 (1976)

Mohd, Iqbal Ahmed -V- state of A.P., A.I.R 1979, G.C.677, 1979, Cr.L.J. 633, 1979

Mohammed Abdul Salam -V- State of Assam, (1988)2 (NOC)33

Moolraj -V- State (1955) Cr. L.J. 1965, Him. Pra.57

M. Karunanidhi -V- Union of India (1973)3 S.C.R. 254,3,. .C.C. 431(1979) S.C.C.(Cri,) 691 (1979), 1979 Cr.L.J. 773

Narayan -V- State (1956) Cr.L.J. 227, A.I.R. 1956, Madh. B.51

Nanak Chand -V- State of Himachal Pradesh, A.I.R 1974, Cr.L.J. 606

Nimeon Sangma -V- Govt.of Meghalaya, 1979, Cr.L.J. 941(S.C.)

Nirmalendu Biswas -V- State (Through the Delhi Special Police Establishment), Criminal Appeal No. 92 of 1979, G .L.R. (NOC) (1987)2

N. Brahmoswara Rao-V- sub-Inspector of Police, Vimkanda, 1978, Cr.L.J 1005 (A.P.)

Navantib Lal -V- Income tax Appellate Assistant Commissioner, 1965, A.S.C. 1375

Om Prakash -V- State of Delhi, A.I.R. 1974, S.C. 989

Osman Mistry -V- Atul Krishna, A.I.R .1949, Calcutta 632

Padam Sen -V- State of U.P. (1961), A.I.R. (S.C.) 218, SC.R.884, Cr.L.J. 322

Pandurang Laxman -V- State of Bombay, A.I..R. 1959. Bombay 30

Prakash Chand -V- State (Delhi Administration), A.I.R. 1979, S.C. 400

Prabhash Kumar Sec - V- The State, Criminal Appeal No. 85 of 1953

Prafulla Chandra Mech -V- Delhi Special

Police Establishment, C.I.A.(II), New Delhi

Prem Kumar -V- State of Punjab (1978) CLR 366 (Punj)

Prithi Raj -V- State of Haryana, 1981, Cr.L.J. 984 (P and H)

Rampukar Singh -V- State, 1981, Cr.L.L. 1631

Ran Pitkar Singh -v- State, A.I.R, 1954, All. 234, 1954 Cr.L.J. 459

Ram Kishore -V- State (1987)31 D.T. 312

Ranjeet Singh -V- State (1957) Cr.L.J. 42(All) 1966 A.L.J. 662

Ram Dulare Yadav -V- State of U.P. Cr.L.J, 983 (Allahabad), 1971

Ram Prakash Arora -V- state of Punjab, A.I.R. 1973, G.C. 498

Rao Shiv Bahadur -V- State of Vindhya Pradesh, A.I.R. 1954, S.C. 322

Republic of India -V- Khagendra Nath, 1982, Cr.L.J. 961 (Orissa)

R.S. Nayak -V- A.R. Antulay, A.I.R. 1984, 2 S.C.C. 188

R.G. Jacob -V- Republic of India, A.I.R. 1963, S.C. 550, 1963 (3)S.C.R. 800 (1963)

R.S. Nayak -V- A.R. Antulay, A.I.R. 1986, S.C. 2045, 1986, Cr.L.J.1922

R. Menon -V- Union of India, 1956, MLJ(c) 387

State of U.P. -V- Kapil Deo Shukla, 1972, Cr.L.J. 1214(S.C.)

State of Bihar -V- Uma Shankar, 1981, Cr.L.J. 159 (S.C.)

State of Maharashtra -V- Pollonji, Darabshow Daruwalla (1988) A.I.R., 1988, S.C. 88

C.A. Venkataraman -V- The State, A.I.R . 1958, S.C. 107, 1958 S.C.J. 594, 1968 S.C.R. 1037

State -V- Pandyrang Bubarao, A.I.R. 1955, Bombay 460

Surajmal -V- State (Delhi Administration,) A.I.R. 1979, S.C. 1408, 1980 (mad. L.J.-Cr.) 73(1979)2 S.C.I. 516, 1979 Cr.L.R.(S.C)717, 1979 (Cr.L.J) 1087, 1979 Cur.L.J. -Cr.) 155, 1979 U.J. (S.C.) 916, 1979 S.C. Cr.R. 313

State -V-Minaketan Patniak (1952) Cr.L.J. 139. A.I.R. 1952, Orissa 267

State -V- Abhey Singh (1957) Cr.L.J. 541, A.I.R. 1957, Raj 138, 1958 Ker. 136

State of Madres -V- A Vaidyenath, Iyer (A.I.R. 1958, S.C.61)

State of Assam- V - Krishna Rao and another, A.I.I. 1973, S.C.28

State of Rajasthan -V- Mohammad Habib, A.I.R. 1973 Cr.L.J. 703

State of UP. -V- Dr G.K. Ghosh, A.I.R. 1948, S.C. 1452, 1983 All. L.J. 1170

S.K. Kale -V- State of Maharastra, A.I.R. 1977, S.C. 822,1977, .Cr.L.J. 604 150

State of Maharastra - V - Kaliar Kail Subramanium Ramaswami, A.I.R. 1977, S.C. Cr.R. 336 1977 Cr.L.S.C.S.C.) 372

Sudhendra Kumar Bhattacharyya -V- State (Delhi Special Police Establishment, 1987) G.L.R. 80

State of Bihar -V- Baswan Singh, 1958, C.500, 1956 B.L.R 818, 1958 Cr.L.J. 970

S.P Bhatnagar -V- State of Maharastra (1979)1 S.C.C. 535

State of karnataka -V- Maniswami and others, A.I.R. 1977, S.C. 822 169

Tara Prasad Banerjee-V- State of Bihar, 1973 Patna L.J.R. 533

The State of Assam -v- Reba Nath Bhattcharyya (1986)2 G.L.R. 70, Criminal Revision No. 128 of 1976

V.V. Joshi -V- State, A.I.R. 1968 Punjab 120

Ved Prakash Goel -V- P. Bania, S.P., C.M.'s Vigilence Cell, Dispur (1983)1 G.L.R. (NOC) 17

V. Narayanan Namibiar -V- State of Kerela, A.I.R, 1968, S.C. 116

Wasanta -V- State of Maharastra, 1984, Cr.L.J. 410 (Bom.)

Prolegomena

For quite a few years there has been an increasing clamour against corruption in India. The criminalisation of socio-economic life have come to the fore which has assumed menacing proportion as underlined by various scams and media reports. Even the Prime Minister and parliament both have acknowledged the fact. An efficient and clearcut policy for legislation against corruption is needed as the type of crime is more dangerous not only because the financial stakes are higher, but also because they cause irreparable damage to public morals.

The trend of corruption amongst rich and influential in India in the last decade is very alarming. The top political leaders as well as the bureaucrats are involved in various types of scams. The word scam has become endemic to our political system. At any rate, 1996 can easily be labelled as the year of scams. (*The Lawyers Collective*, December, 1996-97).

Political entrepreneur flourish or perish according to the quantities of public resources they control and the way they use their resources. Yet the patron has always to maintain the edge between, possession and expenditure of the resources they control. The politicians in power give away the resources more in the form of personalised favour than conserve it. It is the duty of the political entrepreneurs to divert the flow of resources from state agencies to private citizens.

The Home Minister comrade Indrajit Gupta, on his first visit after taking oath to Calcutta called for a national campaign against corruption. In his opinion one should proceed in the matter by setting up citizens committee. On the same day T.N. Seshan, the Chief Election Commissioner appealed at a meetting of big industrialists in Calcutta for launching the second phase of our freedom struggle with the objective of eradicating corruption. Political leaders both at the centre as well as in States since Independence categorically speaking of waging struggle against corruption. The then Prime Minister Deve Gowda too has announced his government's firm position against corruption and criminalisation. India is now ranks among most corrupt countries of the World. We are in the same category as Argentina, Brazil, South Korea, The Philippines. A country where honesty and morality of the Ministers, M.P.s, M.L.As, and Bureaucrate are in question, all the misdeeds and corruption are not pathetic consequence, but natural for that country. It is quite unfortunate that a former Prime Minister, N. Rao has to approach the court to exempt him from personally appearing in a case involving Section 420 of the Cr. P.C. where necessary investigation are not conducted into the repeated allegation of violation of law by the family members of the same personality. The countless erstwhile Ministers are charged with having earned money through unfair means. Had the erstwhile leaders, executives and other personalities in power and privilege in Independent India were free from corruption and sincere in preserving morality and justice and honesty, the country would not destroy and lead to such a pathetic position.

The incidence of corruption has spread everywhere. It has affected everyone, almost all parties by and large. Violation of law and misuse of power are the source of corruption. Accepting money in exchange of granting the advantage, inaction in investigation, disorderly conduct of trial are come of the antisocial activities practiced by dishonest personalities in politics enjoying power and privileges. Another great advantage granted to these personalities directly or indirectly by the statute is that persons enjoying power and pelf do not have to answer for their misdeeds. Corruption in our country has turned into a norm of life and one has got accustomed to the situation. The most alarming situation prevalent in this time is the people's lack of confidence. No political party in India could succeed in erecting a new society free from corruption, injustice, division of class, caste and religion. The causes of failure are manifold. However at least one of the reasons is alround corruption and misuse of power. The honest leaders and workers, and the common people must have protested the corrupt activities of dishonest leaders. But they could not collectively prevent the party's decay due collapse of internal legal framework of the party. Unfortunately the political parties of our country even the leftist have failed to draw the lesson of consequences of the past. The Congress governments have already lost their credibility having been listed the leaders one after another as accusers in financial scams.

The bribes offered by the Bofors Company of Sweden do get a defence contract was accepted by the Ministry. The Harshad Mehta, the Hitens, the Krishnamurthy, the Venkitaramanas and the Ambanis looted at least Rs.10,000 crores through forgeries with political indulgence. The international sugar barons secured additional profits through advance information of imports from Kalpanath Rai, the then Union Minister. In return the Ministers and bureaucrats collected handsome money for their individual profit. With a view to fulfilling the motive of earning money through supply of equipments by a Hyderabad-based firm, despite the fact that it had furnished highest price quotation, Sukh Ram removed the honest officials and posted his own men and women in their places. Crores of rupees earned in the process. In all these processes of looting money, the Ministers, the Bureaucrats and Businessmen are involved.

The States also are not lagging behind and staggering corruption paralelly with the Central Ministers. LOC scam of Rs. 200 crores in Assam', T.V. sets purchase at the highest price lossing Rs. 8.53 crores by the former Chief Minister of Tamil Nadu, J. Jaylalitha, Enron Project case of Maharashtra involving roughly $ 30 billion over the open of 20 years agreement, the Fodder scam of Bihar government headed by Laloo Prasad Yadav are a few of the severe corruption cases detected in States. However it is good sign for us that the courts fight political corruption during 1996 as never before. The Supreme Court, Delhi High Court and lower court Judges and lawyers while attending the Golden Jubilee celebration of the constitution of Constituent Assembly at Vigyan Bhavan at New Delhi expressed their valuable remarks in unusually good spirits against political corruption. In the same function, the President of India, Dr Sankar Dayal Sharma said that, in a climate in which most politicians would like to curtail the power of judges, there was at least one man at the top who could be expected to resist the attempts to strait jacket them. The Chief Metropolitan magistrate Prem Kumar said, while trying the Lakhubhai Pathak case, "Various scams show the unholy nexus of politicians, power brokers, bureaucrats and businessmen in debasing and devaluing the moral authority of our political system. But time is no respect of persons. The basic tenet of the rule of law is : "be you ever so high, the law is above you." During the year 1996 alone a good number of corruption cases of top politicians in power tried abiding by the status and position of judiciary. The important corruption cases against which trials are initiated during the year are - Urea scandal involving 1.33 crores of the former Union Minister Ram Lakhan Yadav, Illegal allotment of 2000 government houses by Sheila Kaul and P.K. Thangoon- former Ministers of Urban development, Hawala cases of receiving Hawla money from the industrialist S.K. Jain by a good number of Narasimha Rao government, JMM case involving some Union

Ministers of Narasimha Rao government, Lakhubhai Pathak case involving the Prime Minister himself and others transacting illegal money of $100000 through the Godman Chandraswami, St. Kitts Affair of the central government.

It is a matter of regret that the Prevention of Corruption Act does not cover the corrupt politicians. By exclusions of corrupt politicians from the purview of the Prevention of Corruption Act indirectly given free hand to corrupt politicians to do corrupt practices for personal gain. Last fortnight, M.P.s of *most* political parties wished not to be termed public servant, because it brings them under the purview of the PC Act. A senior judge of the Supreme Court said - "This is the only way left for them to legalise their looting". Politicians need money for promoting themselves in politics, businessmen need the patronage of persons in the government to become millionaire easily and quickly by offering hard cash each and other services to them. In the system both patronise criminals, to get the unlawful things done smoothly. This nexus is an open secret.

Corruption, no doubt, is a global phenomenon, but all existing systems have adaptability to weed it out. But the Indian democracy is inapt to respond quickly to scams and the caucuses which protect such practices. Many Prime Ministers in Japan resigned because of their involvement in bribery scandals, the U.S. President had resigned for their involvement in the Watergate scandal. But India is not included in such list. The Indian democracy is indebted to the independent judiciary which has passed judgements related to Lakhubhai Pathak cheating case, Jharkhand Mukti Morcha M.P.s pay off, St. Kitts conspiracy, Arms Telecom scandal.

The scams of the recent past have significant contributions towards rapid deterioration of economic health of the country as a whole. The scams involving more than crores of rupees are -

Bank Security Scam	—	Rs. 7000 crores
Hawla Scam	—	Rs. 65 crores
Animal Husbandry Scam	—	Rs. 950 crores
Urea Scam	—	Rs. 133 crores
Sugar Scam	—	Rs. 600 crores
Air Bus Scam	—	Rs. 1200 crores
Medical Equipment Scam	—	Rs. 1000 crores
Arms Telecom Scam	—	Rs. 1.6 crores

Misuse of power for corruption is a common phenomenon among the people having power to deal with resources and money. Absolute power corrupt absolutely. In order to check corruption effectively, much remains to be done positively and constructively. Amendments of relevant provisions in the Prevention of Corruption Act so as to bring the corrupt politicians to the legal net is one of the essential steps of positive action. Boycot of corrupt politicians and officials from the society, imposing restrictions in election, introduction of code of conduct for politicians are some other steps required for control of corruption at least to a significant extent if not completely.

In The Hawala Net

The case deals with persons in power receiving huge amounts of money, not by way of legal remuneration, but by passing the official foreign exchange channels.

Major Accused

Mr. Balaram Jakhar	—	Rs. 83.24 Lakh
Mr. Devi Lal	—	Rs. 1 Lakh
Mr. Pradeep Singh	—	Rs. 60 Lakh (Rs. 35 lakh as public Servant)
Mr. L.K. Advani	—	Rs. 71.50 lakhs (Rs. 51.50 lakhs as Public Servant)

Mr. Kalpanath Rai	—	Rs. 71.50 lakhs (Rs. 51.50 lakh as Public Servant)
Mr. Arjun Singh	—	Rs. 10.50 lakhs
Mr. Yashwant Sinha	—	Rs. 21.80 lakhs
Mr. Arif Khan	—	Rs. 6.50 crores

Mr. N.D. Tiwari and several ether public servants were charged under S.19 of Prevention of Corruption Act. 1988 and under 3.173(8) Cr.P.C.

The Jain brothers were charge sheeted under S.12 of PCA, 1988.

Conspiracy at St. Kitts

Fabrication of bank accounts of the former Prime Minister V.P. Singh and his son Ajeya Singh at St.. Kitts in order to turnish his image has investigated by the CBI and has charge sheeted the former prime minister P.V.N. Rao, former union Minister K.K. Tiwari, the Godman Chandraswami and his secretary Mamaji. It was alleged that Rao, in conspiracy with others forged certain documents to open a bank account in St. Kitts Island in Ajeya Singh's name.

Fodder Scam

This is an another scam in the series involving Rs. 950 crores and the people involved are of very high political standing. Former Bihar Chief Minister and present Railway Minister of India Laloo Prasad Yadav, his key aids Janata Dal MLA, R.K. Rana and Congress MLA Jagdish Sharma were key beneficiaries of this scam. Even former Union Minister Jagannath Mishra and Animal husbandry minister Chandra Deo Prasad Verma were interogated by CBI.

In this scam senior Bureaucrats and politicians conspired to pay of government funds based on fictitious bills for non-existent purchases by the Animal Husbandry Department (AHD) of fodder, medicine of artificial insemination equipment in the four south Bihar districts of Chaibasa, Dumka, Ranchi and Jamshedpur (now in Jharkhand state).

Prosecution of C.M.

With the announcement of then CBI Director, Joginder Singh's decision to prosecute the C.M. Laloo Prasad Yadav and other 56 persons, it opened up the possibility of Laloo Prasad Yadav becoming the first C.M. to face the prospect of being jailed while still in office.

After waiting for 38 days the Bihar Governor A.R. Kidwai at last gave permission to CBI for prosecution of Bihar C.M. and his two colleagues after studying the 1200 pages charge sheet (running into four volumes relating to the case No. RC 20/96).

JMM MPs Pay Off Case

This case was a typical example on political corruption. How money changed the hands to save the minority Government of P.V. Narasimha Rao when completed its five years term being in minority throughout full tenure.

Urea Scam Worth Rs. 1.33 Crores

In this scam a deal was signed between National Fertilizers Ltd. and Karsan, a Turkish Company for two lakh tons of Urea. The money was deposited in various accounts around the world, but India did not receive the delivery of urea. Prabhakar Rao, the son of the former Prime Minister P.V. Narasimha Rao, Sanjeeva Rao and Prakash Chandra, the son or former Fertilizer Minister were involved in this scam like other scams. The outcome of this was also same due to procedural delay, India could not get extradition of Karsan executives and India does not have a treaty with Geneva.

Petrol Pump Allotment Scam

Capt. Satish Sharma who was then Petrolium Minister in the Central Government allotted Petrol pumps and Gas

Agencies to political bigwigs and their relatives. That includes daughter-in-law of former Prime Minister, H.D. Deve Gowda. This shows political favouritism and nepotism, how -Petrol Pumps and Gas Agencies were allotted out of turn from Minister's discretionary quotas.

Petrol Pump allotment scam rocked India's parliament. The latest in an unending series of scandals involving official corruption, the opposition has termed it the largest ever scam in Indian history, involving Rs. 25 billion (US $ 520 million). That much money has changed hands in allotment of Petrol Pumps to supporters of the ruling BJP. The scam involves allotment of a total of 1144 petrol pumps, 1788 LPG and 236 Kerosene oil Agencies across the country. Stung by the public criticism, the Prime Minister on Monday the 5th August, 2002 cancelled all allotments of petrol pumps and allied dealerships since 2000, when the NDA Govt. came to power.

Taj Heritage Corridor Scam

In this scam a huge amount worth Rs. 175 crore were involved. The CBI had lodged the FIR against Mayawati, the C.M. of U.P. and seven others in October, 2003 following directions of the Apex Court. The other accused in the case are Mayawati's party colleague and former Environment Minister of U.P. Hasimuddin Siddique and a battery of U.P.'a top bureaucrates including former Chief Secretary, D.S. Bagga, P.L. Punia who served as Principal Secretary to Mayawati and R.K. Sharma, the State's Environment Secretary Mayawati was also implicated for the disproportionate assets after this Taj Corridor Scam she had properties worth crores of rupees in different towns of U.P. in the name of her brothers, cousins and other relatives. She alleged that this is politically motivated vendetta against her to trouble Dalit's daughter.

Fake Stamp Paper Scam

This scam has broken all the records involving an approximate amount of Rs. 31,000 crores. In this scam fake stamp papers were printed and circulated in the market by one Mr. Abdul Karim Telgi and his aids with the patronage of political bigwigs and senior police officials.

We find the picture of scams which were unearthed, but there might be many which could not be unearthed. In reality the outcome or conviction rate of these high level white collar criminals is very less, when a new scam is brought to the light of public by senior public officials, or when a new Govt. in Centre or State changes hand, the fallout may be some new scams or irregularities done by previous government come to the picture. They become the highlights and headline of all leading news channels and newspapers, but only for few days.

Socio-economic Offences in Corporate Sector

Business houses and industries came forward to help the parties financially in order to have influence over decision making process and corner licences, permits and government facilities at concessional rates if they were in power or whenever they come to attain it. They helped the opposition parties even if they had no prospect of attaining power to keep them in humour so that they did not attack them inside or outside the legislature and did not give a call for a strike by their trade union wings. There are innumerable cases of such type of corruption.

In 1992 Harhat Mehta sent the share prices skyrocketing luring the gullible investors to buy shares and get rich overnight. The fictitious trading ring came to light and the Bank found themselves cheated of $ 1.4 billion.

In 1995 Pawan Sachdeva, Chief of MS Shoes East, a little known company of Delhi spurred more or less similar crisis, with a $ 4.3 million default.

Corporate crimes lead to killing, injuring, maiming and robbing. As for instance Dhori and Chasnala coal mine disasters; where negligence of management as regards safety measures led to the deaths of a large number of people. This incident is the outcome of the desire of the company to minimise its costs and increase its profits, indulging in marketing of substandard and adulterated products by the public servants including top political leaders in order to increase profits by the businessmen sometimes lead to deaths. For example, substandard pressure stoves, LPG cooking ovens with defective regulators, substandard electric gadgets and so on cost many lives.

Corruption in Education Sector

Neither educational bureaucracy nor are the politicians interested in making the government-run schools work effectively because this will make private teaching shops that go by the name of "public schools" redundant. In reality such teaching shops are directly or indirectly run by private businessmen in collaboration with education bureaucracy and politicians and they share in extortion of money from parents and teachers.

Now-a-days the private schools have become the lucrative business. The licences are granted to run the private schools by flouting all the rules and regulations which lack in basic infrastructure and amenities. Even some private schools are run in very crowded localities without any playground and parks.

According to *The Times of India* (August 20, 1997, the major findings of inspection made by the Directorate of the Delhi government in sixteen private "public schools are-

(i) indulging in extortion of money from students on various counts.

(ii) The Delhi Public School Society is opening schools even outside Delhi with the money collected from the Delhi students,

(iii) Some schools have mortgaged school land and building to public and private enterprises and banks to generate money for their respective societies. The interest on the loans taken by the individual society from these enterprises and banks is being paid by the school.

(iv) Some societies and trusts managing schools have given loan to the schools at an interest rate of 21 per cent.

(v) Most schools are collecting huge sums by selling thousands of admission forms, the price of these ranges from Rs. 50.00 to Rs. 250.00. They should not be more than Rs. 10.00 each.

(vi) Collection or huge amounts in the name of admission fee ranging from Rs.1000.00 to Rs.5,000.00. It may go even up to RS. 8000.00 as in some private schools of Assam. The admission fee should not be more than 200.00

(vii) Huge amounts are being collected in the name of security or caution money at admission time, ranging from Rs.1000.00 to Rs.8000.00. It should not be more than Rs.500.00. This amount either not refunded or if it is refunded then it is returned without any interest.

(viii) Schools collect science fee every month from all students without having separate laboratories for secondary and middle classes. Science is one of the subjects in the syllabus and hence there is no question of a separate science fee.

(ix) In some schools a building fund is being collected even though the building is complete in every respect.

(x) Many schools are transferring surplus funds to their respective societies, which if retained in school would enable the managing committee to lower the fee structure and to provide better facilities and staff.

The cases referred here are only few instances of corruption in public life, various mechanisms are being used by the public servants to extort money from all possible sources.

1

Corruption: An Introduction

The Concept

Corruption typically connotes the abuse of public office for personal gain which is usually, but by no means always pecuniary. The legal definition of corruption is by no means confined to the abuse of public office, though this may be viewed more seriously to attract a prosecution. Any employee who corruptly accepts gift as an inducement for doing or refraining from doing anything in relation to his employer's business affairs commits an offence, as does anyone who corruptly offers or provides such gifts.[1] In its widest connotation corruption includes all kinds of improper conduct, whether in the exercise of power or influence attached to a public officer, or in the exercise of social position or influence of one's authority in public life or in the exercise or adoption of personal discretion in conduct in the course of one's business or profession. The problem of corruption is complex having roots and ramifications in society as a whole.

After the World War II, corruption amongst public servants posed a serious problem to the Government and it was realised that existing law in the Indian Penal Code relating to bribery and corruption amongst public servants was wholly inadequate to meet the exigencies of the time. Section 161 of the Indian Penal Code deals with offences committed by public servants by taking gratification other than legal remuneration in respect of an official act. Section 161 says — "Whoever being or expecting to be a public servant accepts or obtains or agrees to obtain or accept or attempts to obtain from any person for himself or for any other person, any gratification whatever, other than legal remuneration, as a motive or reward for doing or forbearing to do any official act or for showing or forbearing to show, in the exercise of his official functions, favour or disfavour to any person, or for rendering or attempting to render any service or disservice to any person with the central or any State Government or Parliament or the Legislature of any State, or with any local authority, corporation or Government company referred to in section 21 or with any public servant, as such, shall be punished with imprisonment of either description for a term winch may extend to three years or with fine or with both.[2] This Section is intended to prevent public servants from taking bribes in any shape whatsoever. Similarly Sec. 165 of the I.P.C. prohibited public servants from taking presents just as they are prohibited from taking any gratification under Sec. 161. The provision of the I.P.C. under Sec. 161 and Sec. 165 are suitable to control corruption. But, the social and economic value system in India has changed to such a large extent during last 57 years of freedom that in many respects the Code does not truly reflect the needs of the present day. After an incisive scrutiny of the working efficiency of the I.P.C, the Santhanam Committee on Prevention of Corruption, 1962 recommended for amendment of provisions under Sec. 21. Recommendations were also made by the Committee for amendment of Sec. 5 of "The Prevention of Corruption Act, 1947."

Corruption cannot be eliminated or even significantly reduced unless preventive measures are planned and implemented in a sustained and effective manner. Preventive measures must include administrative, legal, social, economic and educative measures. Such measures are to be aimed at preventing or reducing corruption not only of the common forms, but also other forms of the evil that are coming into existence to the ever increasing complexities of modern society. It is not possible to evaluate an effective theory of combating corruption without understanding its root cause and mechanism of proliferation of corruption at various social strata, like a disease it has caused factors and symptoms. Preventive measures of corruption must be developed to destroy or discourse the causal factors.

Dimensions

Corruption is not a new offence in our country. It existed in India or elsewhere since ancient time. Kautilya in his Arthasastra refers to the various forms of corruption prevalent in his times. Corruption existed in other countries of the world also, similar to India. Paul. H. Douglas, Senator from Illinois pointed out in his book on "Ethics of Government" that corruption was rife in British public life till a hundred years ago and in U.S.A. till the beginning of last century. But, it has observed that in spite of continuous efforts given to prevent corruption by societies since primitive time generating public authority from minimum in early days to maximum in modern days, corruption has been increasing in a geometrical progression throughout the days. In early days the scope of public authority was minimum. Many of the matters that were looked after by the community have now become a function of the State. The modern conception of integrity of public servants in the sense that they should not use their official position to obtain any kind of financial or other advantage for themselves, their families or friends is due to the development of the rule of law and the evolution of a large permanent public service. Levy of taxation by law, parliamentary control of expenditure and the regulation of conduct of public servants by rules, the breach of which would subject them to penalties including dismissal and prosecution in courts contributed to the present notion of integrity of public servants. The fact that fair, honest and just principles are adopted and declared in matters like recruitment, promotions, terminal benefits and other conditions of service of public services has further encouraged the growth of the currently accented standards of integrity.[3]

Corruption is confined not only to a particular level of officials or workers, it also extends to all levels from top to bottom. The unconscious sanction of corruption at various levels is the outcome of some important factors out of which rise of the get-rich-quick politicians earning of money and wealth by dishonest employees of Government, Semi-Government and Private organisations and high taxation leading to temptation to bribe or to take bribes are prominent. In our country bribe taken by a peon is called "bakshish" and clerk "mamooli." It is *rishwat* or *utkoch* when accepted by a senior official. A Minister takes it in the name of "party funds". Some clever officials raise frivolous objections or queries to deliberately delay matters. Ultimately public are harassed by such unscrupulous officials in every sphere of life. Bureaucratic corruption in India appeared since third century B.C. In a sense corruption is perennial and ubiquitous to be found in any and all systems of government. The problem therefore is not to account for its presence, but rather for its extent in a specific situation at a particular time.

Legal Provisions

The Prevention of Corruption Act, 1947 provides ample power to the administrative machinery to prosecute and book those who are involved in corruption. Sec. 3 of the Act deals with offences under Sec. 165-A of the Indian Penal Code to be cognizable offence. Sec. 4 interprets presumption where public servant accepts gratification other than legal remunerations, Sec. 5 defines criminal misconduct in discharge of official duty, Sec. 6 to 8 provides the procedural part and material requirement for prosecution of offenders. Sec, 405 and 409 of the Indian Penal Code deals with criminal breach of trust by public servant and punishment against the offence.

Conduct Rules and Disciplinary Rules

Different categories of government servants are governed by separate, but substantially similar sets of conduct rules. Similar to Central government services rules, the following sets of rules are in force for Assam Government services.

1. The Assam Civil Services (Conduct) Rules, 1965.
2. The Assam Services (Discipline and Appeal) Rules, 1964.

Framing up of Conduct Rules by the Government indicates that the Government is sufficiently aware of the possible manifestations of corruption and were doing all they could, consistent with the spirit of the times, to combat the evil.

Similar to "All India Services (Discipline and Appeal) Rules, 1955", "The Assam Services (Discipline and Appeal) Rules, 1984 were framed UP BY the Government of Assam to take disciplinary action against corrupt civil servants against whom allegations have been conclusively proved. The Assam Services (Discipline and Appeal) Rules, 1964, prescribed penalties and procedures or their imposition.

Preventive Measures

Corruption cannot be eliminated or even substantially reduced unless preventive measures are planned and implemented in a sustained and effective manner. Preventive action includes administrative, legal, social, economic and educative measures. The aim of introducing preventive measures against corruption is to eliminate the basic causes of its occurrence. The prevailing causes appears to be are —

(1) administrative delays (2) unmanageable regulatory functions undertaken by the Government (3) scope for personal discretion (4) cumbersome office procedures and (5) lack of public consciousness.

Quite often delay is deliberately contrived so as to obtain some kind of illegal gratification. A positive step to reduce administrative delay to the utmost extent is required. The regulatory machinery of the Government seems to be overburdened in maximum cases causing inefficiency in taking timely adequate and appropriate actions against delinquent Civil servants. So, a thorough examination of such matters and planning for effective machinery system is required to prevent corruption. There are sufficient scope for harassment, malpractices and corruption while exercising discretionary powers by different categories of government servants of doubtful integrity and honesty.

So, it is necessary to devise adequate methods of control over exercise of discretionary powers. Cumbersome office procedures also is responsible to encourage corruption amongst public servants. So, a suitable reform on the existing procedures to reduce intervention of touts and intermediaries is imperative. Socio-economic offences like corruption may be prevented by generating public consciousness and brought home through sustained efforts of press, platform and persons. Mere public policy and police agency cannot deliver goods.

Special Police Establishment

Both Central and State Government have a number of establishments to deal with corruption. The Delhi Special Police Establishment has been functioning under the Central Government and its jurisdiction extends to all the States and Union Territories. On the establishment of the Central Bureau of Investigation from 1st April, 1963, the Special Police Establishment has been made one of its division. The Special

Police Establishment has been made as a special agency for making inquiries and investigations into certain specified offences. It is supplementary to the State Police forces. It enjoys with the respective State Police forces concurrent powers of investigation and prosecution in respect of offences notified under Sec. 3 of the Delhi Special Police Establishment Act, 1946.

Vigilance Organisations

In addition to Police Establishments, vigilance organisations, at the centre as well as in States are functioning for implementing anti-corruption activities. In Assam, the following organisations are available to deal with anti-corruption laws.

1. Vigilance and Anti-Corruption Department

This organisation was set up in Assam in the year 1946-47 to deal with corruption amongst public servants. The Vigilance and Anti-corruption department is an agency for making inquiries and investigations into corruption cases against public servants.

2. Chief Minister's Vigilance Cell

This is a special unit attached with the Chief Minister of Assam created in the year 1974 to deal with corruption cases against public servants. This cell is functioning under the direct control of the Chief Minister.

3. Bureau of Investigation of Socio-Economic Offences

This organisation was set up in the year 1975 with a view to investigate socio-economic offences committed through tax evasion. Under item No. 19 of the 20-point programme with the charter of duties to check smuggling activities, hoarders and evasion of taxes and circulation of black money, this establishment has been created. The Bureau of Investigation of Socio-Economic offences is functioning under the direct control of Political Department with the offices from Police department and other concerning departments of the state, that is Tax officials, Forest department, Transport department, Agriculture department, supply department etc.

4. Lokayukta

Lokayukta is an establishment created as per provision of The Assam Lokayukta and Up-Lokayukta Act, 1985. The provision for appointment of Lokayukta and Up-Lokayukta has been made in the Act. for the investigation of grievances and allegations against Ministers, Legislators and other public servants in certain cases and for matters connected therewith. The Act extends to the whole of the State of Assam and applies also to the public servants posted outside Assam in connection with the affairs of the State of Assam. For the purpose of conducting investigations, in accordance with the provisions of this Act, the Governor shall by warrant under the hand and seal appoint a person to be known as the Lokayukta and one or more persons to be known as the Up-Lokayukta or Up-Lokayuktas. The Up-Lokayuktas shall be subject to the administrative control of the Lokayukta and in particular, for the purpose of convenient disposal of investigations under this Act. The Lokayukta shall be a person who is or has been a Judge of the Supreme Court or a High Court and the Lokayukta or Up-Lokayukta shall be a person who is not and has never been a member of Parliament or a member of the Legislature of any State and shall not hold any office of trust or profit. The term of the Office of the Lokayukta or Up-Lokayukta is five years or 68 years of age, whichever is earlier.

The trial of corrupt public servants are being made exclusively by the Court of Special Justice.

Trend of Corruption in Assam

Throughout the period of study, the corruption in Assam

is perhaps not less staggering than any other State in India. All the diverse organs of the State Government has carried a traditional association with corrupt practices in different forms and decrees. The prevention and control of corruption even tightening with stringent laws becomes ineffective due to increasing complicacy of the mechanism of corruption. As a result its dimension has been widening instead of narrowing.

Impact of Anti-Corruption Laws

Creation of a social climate both among the public servants and in the general public in which bribery, illegal gratification and corruption in *any* other form may not flourish is perhaps be a strong measure to fight corruption in public life. The law can only define a corrupt practice. The law-enforcer can only apprehend and the law courts can only punish those brought before it. But, the corrupt are too many and their accomplices too large in number. The ingenuities of these Artful Dodgers are simply stupendous, Only a few in the proportion of the corrupt are caught in the legal net. The society itself has to wage a war against corruption membership.

It is not possible to investigate mathematically, the exact extent and number of corruption incidences. But, its gravity and nature is so acute, that the overall situation of the problem creates extreme complicacy to the Administration. By stocking the trend and extent of corruption and control measures so far taken by law enforcement machineries, some uptodate means and methodology of its control can be evaluated. The present investigation is aimed at cutting that Gordian Knot.

The Prevention of Corruption Act, 1988

With a view to strengthening the provisions of the Prevention of Corruption Act, 1947 and to make the existing anti-corruption laws more effective, the Prevention of Corruption Act, 1947 has been repealed in 1988. The Prevention of Corruption Act, 1947 was amended in 1964 based on the recommendations of the Santhanam Committee. There are provisions in Chapter IX of the Indian Penal Code to deal with public servants and those who abet them by way of criminal misconduct. There are also provisions in the Criminal Law Amendment Ordinance, 1944, to enable attachment of ill-gotten wealth obtained through corrupt means, including from transferees of such wealth. All the provisions have been incorporated in the repealed Act of 1988 with modifications so as to make the provisions more effective in combating; corruption among public servants. The Act of 1988 envisages widening the scope of the definition of the expression "public servant", incorporation of offences under Sec. 161 to 165-A of the I.P.C. enhancement of penalties provided for these offences and incorporation of a provision that the order of the trial court upholding the grant of sanction for prosecution would be final if it has not already been challenged and the trial has commenced. In order to expedite the proceedings, provisions for day to day trial of cases and prohibitory provisions with regard to grant of stay and exercise of power of revision on interlocutory orders have also been included, since the provisions of Sec. 151 to 165-A are incorporated in the Act with an enhanced punishment, those sections in I.P.C. have been deleted.

The present study covers the period of pre- and post-amendment of the Act.

REFERENCES

1. *Report of the Gaming Board for Great Britain*, 1976; H.C. 253,1977, Paras 46-7 and 1977, H.C. 278,1977, Para 26.
2. Ranchhoddas, R. and Thakore, D.K., *The Indian Penal Code*, 26th Ed., 1987.
3. Ministry of Home Affairs, Government of India, *Committee on Prevention of Corruption*, New Delhi, August, 17, 1963.

2

Incidence of Corruption

Disciplinary Powers and Incidence of Corruption

Creation of a clean and ideal society is possible only by members with strict adherence to a high standard of ethical behaviour. There is sufficient scope for civil servants to remove corruption from the society by efficient and honest discharge of their official duties with a high sense of dedication and integrity. But, it becomes a crying need of our society. The civil servants taking responsibilities of managing the affairs of public interest are not endowed with a high sense of dedication and integrity in equal measure. The scope of exercising power for honest and efficient service is being utilised for selfish ends by different categories of government servants. Scope for personal discretion in the exercise of power vested on them makes the problem more acute. There is scope for harassment, malpractices and corruption in the exercise of discretionary powers.

The civil servants who run the governmental agencies may not be able to change the laws, but they can change the ways the laws are carried out. And although most civil servants who are to exercise their discretionary powers lack the political influence of elected officials, they are free from the focus of public attention and therefore safer targets for corruption. It would not be possible to completely eliminate discretion in the exercise of powers, but it can be reduced to the minimum, by devising a system of administration for exercise of personal discretion consistently with efficiency and speedy disposal of public business. It is necessary in this direction to devise adequate methods of control over exercise of discretion. Such control measures should be on the basis of the needs of the situation.

Corruption Amongst Professionals and Technical Service Personnel

There is a wide scope for professionals to exercise corrupt practices. Professionals and technical personnel are dealing with setters of specialisation on which others have little or no command. As such there is enough scope for those personnel to exercise corrupt practices for their personal gains. On the contrary the illegal activities of professionals have received far less attention. Professional organisations often claim that greater outside supervision would be nothing more than unnecessary meddling in their affairs, because the professions police them -selves being specialised in nature and extent. It is also true that the professional and technical organisations such as lawyers, physicians, engineers, scie-ntists do have great power to regulate their members principally through control of professional licensing. But, when the interest of the public clashes with that of the profession, this power is used repeatedly to protect the profession and its individual practitioners. It is obvious that, professionals who violate criminal law, violate public trust are seldom faced with sancti-ons from the agencies of professional self regulation. Professional groups generally have succeeded in keeping the criminal offences of their members out of the criminal justice system. By their very nature of specialisation, the occupational duties of many professionals are complex and difficult for the outsider to understand. Even in the best of circumstances a criminologist or a police investigator might have considerable difficulties in determining the self-serving actions of a particular practitioner being bad judgement or outright fraud. The Professional mistification is helpful not only to insulate professionals from the outside meddling of the criminal justice system, but from the complaints of their customers as well.

Compared to other workers professionals are enjoying a high degree of individual autonomy, Self regulations give many advantages for the professionals, but few for the general public. Similar to administrators, professionals of self regulation have generally shown great leniency towards the offences against strong sanctions at their disposal.

The problem of corruption stands in acute form in medical and engineering professions. Unnecessary medical procedures are not only costly, but pose a serious threat also to the health and even the life of the patient. The temptation to make extra profits by performing unnecessary procedures is always present. Another threat from medical profession arises due to deliberation in supply and purchase of adulterated drugs from black listed manufacturers. The problem of adulteration of drugs and also of production of spurious and sub-standard drugs are nowadays posing serious threat to the health of the community. Such adulterated and sub-standard drugs are being purchased and supplied to the government health care centres by the officials of health departments to gain profits in terms of commission from the manufacturing companies concerned. Engineering departments are also equally footing in corruption. The procedures and works of such departments are monopolised the profession of technocrats. In a majority of cases, the anxiety to avoid delay has encouraged the growth of dishonest practices like the system of "speed money" which has become a common type of practices particularly in setters relating to the award of contracts etc.[1]

Other professionals like lawyer, accountants, forestry,

veterinary and animal husbandry, fisheries, public health, excise, transport etc. also are practising corruption in a rampant way.

Corruption Amongst Administrators

Administrative delays are one of the major causes of corruption. Quite often delay is deliberately contrived so as to obtain some kind of illicit gratification. Administrative delay must be reduced to the utmost extent possible and firm action should be taken to eliminate all such causes of delays as it provides scope for corrupt practices.[2] Administrators are vested with discretionary powers and its extent limits according to the categories. Discretionary powers are exercised by different categories of government servants having administrative responsibilities. All such government servants are not endowed with a high sense of dedication and integrity in equal measure. In discharging duties with discretionary power, a government servant can act with corrupt motive. There is scope for harassment, malpractices and corruption in the exercise of discretionary powers. Functioning of public office is not a easy task under the prevailing circumstances and at the same time it is not possible to completely eliminate discretion in the exercise of powers. But, it should be possible at any cost to devise a system of administration which would reduce to the minimum. Any reform in administration should be aimed at enhancing efficiency and speed of disposal of public business.

Bureaucratic corruption is as old as government office, we hear of it in Babylon and in Rome, in classical India of the third century B.C., in the, pre-Reformation Catholic Church and in the Spanish. Empire, to come no closer to our own day.[3] In a phase corruption is perennial and ubiquitous, to be found in any and all systems of government. The problem therefore is not to account for its presence, but rather for its extent in a specific situation at a particular time.

As for the Dutch East India Company, an official investigation after its collapse found that, there were very few offices in India whose occupants could exist on the legal income. India has the longest history of anti-corruption work. Eventhough the situation in India on corruption did not improve. Corruption in lower level indirectly ignored by the superiors due to title fact that they are underpaid and there is little or no possibility of the government ever providing them with adequate salaries and petty corruption is tolerated to allow them to make ends meet. But, in case of gazetted officers, the spread of corruption among them has called for counter measures. It has never been alleged that salaries for this group were too low, in the conventional sense of being insufficient to support a customary standard of living. It was rather that the opportunities with which they were presented suddenly proliferated. This first occurred during the second world war, when controls were imposed on the economy. With independence and the coming to power of the Congress Party, they were increased in pursuit of socialist goals. Furthermore the state invaded over more sectors of the economy; the banks for instance were nationalised in the year 1970 by the then Prime Minister of India Indira Gandhi. All this, as might have been predicted, led to a considerable increase in corruption amongst civil servants, it is obvious that the amount of corruption in the administration is less than public belief would follow. In any one year, not more than one per cent of gazetted officers is allowed to be guilty of corruption. The number against whom a case can be established, and who can then be convicted is even smaller. In spite of having establishments to control corruption, it his not teen reduced. For this there seems to be two reasons. First, opportunities continue to abound. To take only a few instances, licenses and permits are required for a great number of activities, contracts have to be placed for supplies, the nationalised banks extend credit to cultivators. Those departments that deal most directly with the economy like the department of finance, Railway, Communications etc. are the most corrupt. The CBI report for 1980 gives details of cases dealt with in the courts. Of 172 convictions, fifty three (31 per cent) were of officials from the ministry of Finance (thirty six being from the public sector banks), twenty five (15 per cent) from the Railways, Twenty one (12 per cent) from the Ministry of Communications (mainly Posts and Telegraphs) and fourteen (8 per cent) from the Ministry of Defence.[4]

Prevention of Corruption in the administration is primarily the responsibility of departmental heads. However their position hardly encourages them to give it absolute priority. Political corruption is also directly or indirectly linked with administrative corruption. Corrupt politicians are unable to demand honesty in their civil servants with any degree of conviction. Rather they serve as a model and an excuse for the corrupt official. And it must regretfully be recorded that political corruption in India is increasing and involves even the very highest levels of government. One cannot therefore expect any policing a effort to come from that quarter. Another lacuna for enhancing corruption in administration is that the administrators have the opportunity to suppress corruption practised by their colleagues. In most of the cases it seems that the administrators are reluctant to take any action against corrupt activities of their subordinate colleagues. Corruption cannot be controlled in a country where administration itself is corrupted.

Under the prevailing system of administration, the number of bureaucrats has increased enormously with the result that decisions are avoided, responsibility shrinked and papers are floated up and down the hierachial ladder, thus delaying decisions and keeping people waiting for unduly long periods. The bureaucracy must be made accountable not only for its actions, but also its inaction in view of the current tendency that safety and profit lie in doing nothing. So, it is necessary to have an inspection agency that would carry out random checks at all levels of the administration to ensure quick disposal of cases and detect corruption and delay at all levels. The present system of job security irrespective of performance is to be modified. Promotion on the basis of seniority alone removes any incentive for outstanding work. Efficiency, honesty, merit and performance are to give more importance than to mere seniority at all levels specially at the higher echelons.

Corruption has existed in the pre-Independence are also in some form or other. After independence the old bureaucratic framework retained. The reason for this is that we were accustomed to this type of administration. In the independent India the people came to tolerate corruption as a normal feature of public life. The unconscious sanction of corruption at various levels of administration is the outcome of some important factors out of which, rise of the get-rich-quick politicians, earning of wealth by dishonest employees and high taxation leading to temptation to bribe or to take bribes are prominent.

Nowadays it is open secret that only a few departmental officers are free from corruption. Public services are polluted with corruption for personal gain without considering for national development.

Political Corruption

The fall of integrity among Ministers are common. Some have enriched themselves illegitimately, obtained good jobs for their sons and relations through favouritism and nepotism. In India's democratic polity, corruption has been a perennially live issue even before the advent of Rajiv Gandhi with his involvement in a series of bribery scandals from Boeing to

Bofors. Morariv Desai as the Deputy Prime Minister in the Indira Gandhi Government was accused of conniving at his son's dubious ways of getting rich quick by trading favours with business houses. The accusers belonged to the ruling Congress Party itself even when they were formally levelled by an opposition politician like Madhu Limaye. Subsequently as the Janata Prime Minister, Desai was put in the dock by his Number Two in the Cabinet, Choudhury Charan Singh. The different Communist factions in Kerala charged one another with corruption and bribery.[5]

Corruption amongst politicians is in existence throughout the world. In Pakistan when Field Marshal Ayub Khan seized power in 1958, the burden of his case against the deposed politicians was that they were corrupt. About a decade later, Zulfiquar Ali Bhutto spearheaded the campaign to out Ayub Khan on a plank of anti-corruption. In 1977, bhutto himself was at the receiving and of malfeasance charges and so was his successor and executioner, General Zia-Ul-haq. The successor of Zia-Ul-Haq, Benazir Bhutto and her political opponents similarly levelled with trade corruption charges with basis. In India also corruption amongst politicians has been a continuous process, there was a subtle, if not ingenious method of collecting bribes perfected by Kasu Brahmananda Reddy, an ex-Governor of Maharashtra and ex-Chief minister of Andhra Pradesh. The late Damodaran Sanjivaih, who was the Congress President tried to prevail upon Indira Gandhi, then Prime Minister of India to drop Reddy, but in vain. In fact he had risen higher in the hierarchy and was made the Union Home Minister before and during the 1975 Emergency. Abdul Rehman Antulay, an ex-Chief Minister of Maharashtra was charged with gross misconduct of corrupt practices during his tenure as Chief Minister, for the period from 1980 till he submitted his resignation on January 12, 1982. It is broadly alleged that the accused who was the Chief Minister of the

State of Maharashtra between the period from August, 1980 to September, 1981 conceived a scheme of aggrandisement involving obtaining of funds from the members of the public and putting them substantially under his own control for the disbursal of the funds so obtained. The complaint proceeded to refer to the setting up of various trusts and alleged that the cornerstone of the scheme involved receipt by the accused of illegal gratification other than legal remuneration as a motive or reward for doing or forebearing to do any official act, or for showing or forebearing to show in the exercise of his official functions, favour or disfavour to persons, or for rendering or attempting to render any service or disservice to such persons who dealt with the State Government in general and with public servants who forced part of the Government. It was specifically alleged that the scheme devised by the accused was a immigrant abuse of his official position as Chief Minister for obtaining control over funds which would be used for purposes conducive to the interest of the accused himself. Not only Prime Ministers, the Union Ministers and other cabinet colleagues of State Governments are not free from corruption except in few rare cases. The variations in voices against corruption of political leaders from State to State seems raised various types of corruption charges against Assam Ministers also levelled from the post though in lenient persuation.

In June, 1962, the Government of India constituted a Committee on prevention of Corruption, headed by K. Santhanam, M.P, In its unanimous report, the Committee found that the ultimate source of corruption were (i) Ministers (ii) Legislators (iii) Political parties and (iv) Industrialists and Merchants who seeks favour from these three. The fall in integrity among Ministers is not uncommon. But the Committee's recommendations regarding these ultimate sources of corruption have not received serious attention,

Black money earned by concealing income for the purpose of tax evasion is growing at a fast rate. According to findings of International Monetary Fund (IMF), the quantum of black money in India is about fifty percent of GNP in 1984 and generating at the rate of rupees two crores per hour. Prof. Kaldor in his report on Indian Tax reform submitted to the Government of India in 1953-54, estimated that the amount of black money was of the order of Rs. 800 crores or six per cent of GNP at market prices. In the sixties, the government instituted The Direct Tax Inquiry Committee (DTEC), popularly known as Wanchoo committee, to have a fresh look at the matter. This Committee mainly adopted the methodology of Kaldor and later submitted its report in 1971. According to DTEC, the amount of black money generated in 1968-69 was of the order of Rs. 1400 Crores (4.2 per cent) of GNP). Another major cause of corruption in India is the use of black money in election by the political parties. The ceiling on election expenses for a Lok Sabha seat is Rs. one lakh, while for a State Assembly seat is Rupees fifty thousand. Sri B.K. Nehru, a seasoned bureaucrat said in a public lecture in 1980: "It was estimated that the cost of an election in a Parliamentary Constituency was Rupees five lakhs, to Rupees twenty lakhs and that in a State Assembly Constituency between Rupees one lakh and Rupees five lakhs. There were 542 elected members to Lok Sabha and 3553 members of State Assemblies. The total cost to the parties and the candidates was colossal. The system has tended to generate into a more direct relationship between the money contributed and the favour granted. Once this nexus was accepted as a valid commitment of the democratic culture, nor even the most powerful leader could stop the advance of corruption."

On the basis of B.K Nehru's lecture the total amount of black money invested in general elections for both Parliamentary and State Assembly seats will be of the order of Rs. 1300 Crores. The then Chief Election Commissioner, S.L. Shakdhar wrote in an article in 1980; It is said that money comes *from* businessmen, big and small, foreign countries and all sorts of questionable sources. It is not *my* purpose to fathom this. Put there is a feeling that elections are tainted with money illegally obtained and this creates a doubt whether elections are indeed free, fair and pure." Those who entered politics must be honest and educated in policy rather they hard put to it to enunciate what the election manifestos of their respective parties. The corrupt politicians are very much interested to sit in legislatures in the persuit of power only, Sri N. Sanjiva Reddy after assuming the office of the President of India in 1978 stated that — "the generation of black money and its related off shoots such as corruption in elections, demoralisation of public services and deterioration of standards in public life should be curbed with a strong Land." The Choksi Committee set up by the government of India on direct taxes has in October, 1978 submitted a voluminous resort covering both substantive and management problems. The Committee has recommended enactment of a single, integrated code to cover the administrative and management of four main direct taxes—income tax, gift tax, wealth tax and surtax on company profits. But, the decision of the Government under the Taxation Laws Act, 1978 to exempt political parties from wealth tax as well as from income tax, keeping aside the recommendations of the Choksi Committee is quite disappointing and Showed a critical biasness The Administrative Reform Commission has considered the question of corruption at the political level. It has suggested a permanent authority to keep a continuous vigilance over Ministers, by setting up a Lokpal on the same model as the "Ombudsman" in the Scandinavian countries. A new Bill should provide that action initiated on the recommendation of the Lokpal should be supervised by an authority independent of the Government.

Corruption at Lower Echelons

It may be concluded that bribery and corruption in present day India is not only widespread, but also is accepted as a normal business practice in many segments of the economy. There is however no reliable way to gauge the true extent of the problem. In India the attitude of the people is one of apathy and can be described in various names. A bribe taken by a peon is called "bakshish" and by a clerk "mamool". At higher level it is called rishwat. The bribe givers are also responsible to the aggravation of the problem, he may not expect anything done unlawfully. But he wants rapid movement of files and quick decisions. Some members of the staff in an office have got into the habit of not doing anything till they are suitably rewarded. Some clever officials and dealing clerks raise frivolous objections or questions of queries to deliberately delay matters. Ultimately public are harassed by such anti-social officials and clerks in every sphere of life.

The main cause of corruption at lower echelon is estimated to be of economic necessity. Economic necessity has encouraged some who could not resist temptation. It is noted that the procedures and practices in the working of government offices are cumbersome and delatory. The anxiety to avoid delay has encouraged the growth of dishonest prectices like the system of speed money. Not only for movement of files, in other mauers also, taking of bribe at lower level and its links with officials upto certain level is a common feature, for corruption is greater and the incentive to corrupt stronger at those points of the organisation where substantive decisions are taken in matters like assessment and collection of taxes, determination of eligibility for obtaining licenses, grant of licenses, ensuring fair utilisation of licenses and goods obtained thereafter, giving of contracts, approval of works and acceptance of supplies. It is not always the Government servant who takes the initiative in the matter, frequently enough it is the dishonest contractors and suppliers who having obtained the contract by undercutting want to deliver inferior goods or get approval for such sub-standard work and for this purpose, are prepared to spend a portion of their ill earned profit. Corruption at lover levels becomes intensive in offices where the controlling officer himself is corrupt and inefficient, An inefficient officer is generally working on dictation of dealing clerks who are over powered the officer due to weakness in rules and procedures. This is specially true where public office is occupied by underqualified, incompetent or even corrupt officials enjoy protection of powerful patrons.

REFERENCES

1. Goswami, D.D. (1983): Administration of; P.W.D. In Assam, Since 1874; Ph.D. Thesis, p. 249.
2. *Report of the Committee on Prevention of Corruption,* (1963), p. 44.
3. Palwier Leslie (1983), *Bureaucratic Corruption and Its Remedies,* p. 207.
4. Michael Clarke (1983), *Corruption, Causes, Consequences and Control,* p. 211.
5. Bhargava, G.S. (1989), *"Political Corruption Mainstream,"* Dec. 30; pp. 15-20.

3

Attitude of People Towards Corruption

Reactions and Responses

It is very much essential to create a social climate both among public servants and in the general public in which bribery and corruption may not flourish. In the long run, the fight against corruption will succeed only to the extent to which a favourable social climate is created. When such social climate is created and people deter corrupt practices and the public servants and social controls becomes effective, other administrative, disciplinary and punitive measures may become unimportant and may be relaxed and reduced to a minimum. There is a large consensus of opinion on the visible cause of corruption that a new tradition of integrity can be established only if the example is set by those who have the ultimate responsibility for the governance of India, namely the Ministers of the Central and State Governments. It is very difficult to achieve this objective under the prevailing climate of the environment where the morality of public servants and public representatives has been degrading.

There is a widespread impression that failure of integrity is not uncommon among Ministers and that some Ministers who have held office during last three decades of independence have enriched themselves illegitimately, obtained good jobs for their sons, daughters and relations through favouritism and nepotism, and have reaped other advantages inconsistent with any notion of purity in public life.

Next to the Ministers, the integrity of members of Parliament and of legislatures in the States will be a great factor in creating a favourable social climate against corruption. In an environment where a nexus between politicians and public developed in the form of a direct relationship between the money contributed and the favour granted in the process of collecting funds for political parties, nobody can stop the advance of corruption. The public belief in the prevalence of corruption at high political levels has been strengthened by the manner in which funds are collected by political parties, especially at the time of elections Such suspicions attach not only to the ruling Party, but also to all parties as often the opposition can also support private vested interests. According to the assessment made by Sri B.K. Nehru, ex-Governor of many States *in* India, in one particular state not less than thirty per cent of the legislators were involved in criminal cases.

The principles of democracy clearly indicates that, the force behind the laws in democracy is the opinion of the common man. But, the people in India seems not so much conscious to grow strong opinion against laws and corruption as in other advanced countries in this respect such as U.S.A., U.K. etc. In spite of the various laws aimed at prevention of profiteering, undeserved incomes reached the hands of businessmen, professionals and serviceman. Although the system should be geared to allow only the incomes to different sections of people, yet secondary efforts have to be made to achieve the object by the system of direct taxation. The main current of opinion has placed much reliance on them for the purpose of rationalising disparities in individual incomes and wealths. Hence the process of taxation involves effectuation of economic justice.

Since the publication of the Wanchoo Committee report on 24th December, 1971, "Black Money" "Parallel Economy" and "Unaccounted Incomes and Wealth" have been a matter of continuous discussion at both political and economic levels and at academic as well as popular gatherings. Inspite of Government's commitment to eradicate the problem of black money, the menace of black *money* not only remain, but also goes on assuming bigger and bigger proportions, posing grave dangers to the country's economy, polity and socio -cultural life. One of the worst consequences of black money and tax evasion is that their pernicious effect on the general moral fibre of society. They put integrity at a discount and place a premium on vulgar and ostentatious display of wealth. Many of the newly rich who enjoy material prosperity and social prestige owe their existence really to anti-social activities.[1]

Corrupt officers are extremely intelligent and know the art of pleasing their bosses and people around then. There are no complaints against such clever officers. In such cases the vigilance officers should initiate suo moto action without waiting for complaint. Corruption is an old disease. Its eradication is not easy, but it can certainly be minimised by removing public apathy, creating strong public opinion against it, and educating the younger generation about the evils of corruption and virtues of honesty.[2] A smuggler, a black marketeer, a hoarder, a mafia gangster, may even a decoit becomes respectable and is accepted by society once he becomes a businessman, a manufacturer, a builder, a film producer, a hotel owner and so on. Politics brings wealth and with money you can cut a miche for yourself in public life.[3] Gandhiji hoped that the pressure of public opinion would curb the tendency of the trading classes to profit out of mass misery. But, in reality such type of public opinion had not been created. The impact of the Gandhi era lasted several years after independence. Even the slightest manifestation of corruption and greed disturbed the followers. It is also true that, the sons and daughters, the grand sons and grand daughters of renowned freedom fighters and their wives and husbands who have reacted sharply against the austerity and self denial of their elders, dead or alive. To fight the corrupt situation of India to-day, it is necessary to organise public opinion, especially among the exploited majority to rise against corruption and its practitioners.[4] It is a question of educating the voter and strengthening his or her will to register resentment.[5]

The issue of economic justice in India has from the time of independence sufficient amount of public opinion and there exists in post independent India an appreciable number of laws dealing either directly or a little indirectly with issues. The issues have occupied a cardinal position in the opinion conflicts of the country. The majority of the poor do not know that economic injustice is being done to them under the present system of economic exploitation.

It is well known that black money breeds more black money at an exponential rate and reaches new areas. This subverts the processes of earning an honest and decent living by the majority of our people through inflation, misdirection of investment etc. Just as it lines the pockets of a small fraction of society. The gravity of the problem must be realised by the government as well as by the general public, for its—eradication process. The public expressions appeared in medias so far concentrated mainly on estimating the extent of black incomes and the nature of exploitation, and thereby the concept of the problem remains vague and ambiguous on public record. Any scheme of the Government implemented against black money must be participated by the majority of population for its effectivity. The emphasis on direct taxes has been increasing day by day as effective measures to unearth black money and prevent its proliferation through further evasion. A lot of publicity has been done to encourage people to give taxes in due time. The majority of population does not however understand the implication of modern taxes. In such cases, it cannot be said that these laws are the result of public opinion, That is why the tax evaders continue to enjoy a good status, among the poor, for the purpose of whom taxes are imposed in the final analysis.[6] Direct taxes administration Inquiry Committee set up by the central Government invited opinion of the public on the issues under consideration. Such Committees, which often precede legislation, afford an opportunity to affected section a of society to articulate their views. The Committees suggested inter slim, that names of defaulters should be publicised, evidence in respect of wealth and income submitted by an assessee should be allowed to be used *by* any party, against the submitting party, all assessees should be required to furnish statements of their total assets after each interval of four years, so that any unaccounted addition may be caught. Direct taxes, particularly income tax has started attracting greater attention of the general public, Black Money" has become an accepted fact of social life. Reaction of the people to such measures is mixed. While some criticise the Government for being slack in implementation of these laws, others consider them an unwarranted burden, however, the majority of the masses remains blissfully ignorant of all these phenomenon. Tradesmen organisations nave often called for total withdrawal of direct taxes, as they yield only three percent of the total revenue receipts of the central Government and involve much expenditure.[7] In the race between the tax collector and tax payer, the tax payer has always run ahead and has always succeeded in dodging the tax collector. The tax payer has often sneaked through loopholes in law with the advice of tax consultants, and legislature has done much legislation in vain. There seems to be no apparent reason due to which exemption is granted to the ex-rulers on the annual value of a palace, This shows now sometimes a counter-current of opinion may manage to influence legislation.

It was the feeling of many people that huge amount a of unaccounted incomes may be kept in the form of big denomination notes, that is one thou-sand rupees, five thousand rupees, ten thousand rupees and twenty thousand rupees. The idea of demonetising high denomination notes of rupees one thousand and onwards wee put to test in 1978 by the Janata Government with its high. popularity.[8] The measure received wide public applause, but it was able to unearth only a small fraction of estimated black money. Now, mass opinion in favour of demonetisation of hundred rupee notes received attention. Thus direct tax legislation is affecting more and more public and generating more and store opinion. On the other hand, it is undergoing constant changes to respond to changed social circumstances. The fact that it does not influence rural masses and general masses directly, keeps the sphere of its impact comparatively small. The increasing concern of the public about tax evasion has led to the appointment of Choksi Committee to go into the working of tax laws. The report submitted by Choksi Committee advocated maintenance of present rate of tax.

On the basis of public opinion generated in the country, Company Act of 1956 was passed. The Act contained many provisions to effectuate socio— economic change in line with the aspirations of the people. The main problem in this field was concentration of large sources of income in the hands of a few enterpreneurs have arranged to become chief beneficiaries of corporate system in the country. Many persons in the ruling party were in a favour of drastic changes in the Company Act to avoid concentration of wealth and income in the hands of a few. Many provisions were introduced in the Company Act of 1956 for this purpose. No person can now become a managing director of more than two companies at a time according to Section 316 of the Indian Companies Act, 1956.

The popular sentiment of people against corruption has been responded by the Supreme Court of India while deciding such cases. Provisions in taxing statutes designed to prevent evasion of tax have been upheld as reasonable restrictions on the rights of citizens under Art. 19 (f) (1) and (2) as being in the interest of general public. Thus Ss. 15 (3) (a) (i) and (ii) of the income tax Act, 1361, which imposed on a person a tax in respect of the income earned by his wife and minor child in partnership Business, was reasonable, as it was designed to prevent evasion of tax by carrying on business nominally in the name of a wife and minor child.[9] Similarly, the provision of the Wealth Tax Act, 1957, refusing to recognise a transfer in favour of a wife and minor children living with the assessee where such transfer was not for adequate consideration was upheld as designed to prevent large scale evasion of tex.[10]

In Assam, public response in creating opinion against corruption seems negligible. Corrupt practices by dishonest officials and other personnel have been going on without any resistance. Several such cases detected by Anti-Corruption departments and agencies ultimately failed at certain levels either due to delay in taking action as per procedure or due to undue favour granted by administration.

Redressal

While it is possible to deal quickly with some forms of corruption, it is in general a long-term problem which requires firm resolve and persistent endeavour for many years to come. Unremittingly vigilence is needed to anticipate or at least to spot them as soon as they emerge, and deal with them promptly,[11] Law relating to corruption among public servants has been dealt with in several Acts. Prevention of Corruption Act, 1947 as well as Section 161 to 165-A of Chapter IX of the Indian Penal Code, 1860 provided the more effective prevention of bribery and corruption; while criminal law amendment Act, 1952 enabled a speedier mode for the trial of the offences under the Act of IT of 1947 and Section 161 to 165-A, of I.P.C There were also provisions in the criminal Law ordinance, 1944 to enable attachment of ill-gotten wealth obtained through corrupt means. Now all these provisions have been incorporated in the Prevention of Corruption Act, 1988. In The Prevention of Corruption Act, 1988, apart from consolidating the law on the subject the scope of the definition of the expression "Public Servant" has been widened; penalties provided for the offences have been enhanced; Prosecution has been attached to the order of the trial court upholding the grant of sanction; provisions for day to day trial of cases and prohibitory provisions with regard to grant of stay and exercise of powers of revision on interlocutory orders have also been included.

Corruption is still rampant amongst public servants and there has been enormous increase in bribery and corruption. Thus it is still a great menace to the society. The Prevention of Corruption Act, aims at eradication of this great social evil. But, the cases of bribery and corruption have been fast increasing and polluted the environment of the present day society. So, speedy redressal of such anti-social elements becomes a dire need of the day. Redressal of corrupt public servants with effective implementation of available laws becomes difficult under the prevailing circumstances. Several factors contributed to this problem. At times the members of the community themselves knowingly or unknowingly contribute to the commission of this white collar criminality. Illegal gratifications to public servants and black marketing are some of the common examples where 'victims' of the crimes are also to be blamed for corruption.[12] In fact such crimes cannot be committed unless there are two parties viz. giver end taker are present. The high socio-economic status of corrupt officials also creates problem for redressal. They belong to an influential group which is powerful enough to handle their occupation tact-fully and the persons effected thereby hardly know that they are victimised, the public in general is also somewhat apathetic to such crimes. Thus causing obstruction for prosecution and punishment of such criminals. It is often alleged that the criminal law administrators and judges also belong to upper strata of the society and therefore they generally sympathetic towards white collar criminals while dealing with them. Corrupt public servants close contacts with agencies of social control on account of their social status end privileged positions also creates difficulty for prosecutions and law makers to take appropriate action against them. Many a times these criminals even control the press and are quite friendly with the public and the top ranking public officials. Moreover, the impact of white collar crime falls on such large number of people that it does not aggravate the feelings of one single individual.[13]

In the primitive and medieval societies only few authorities existed to collect taxes, administration of justice or other purposes did not act according to any definite written laws or rules, but largely at their discretion subject to good conscience and equity end directives from the higher authorities, The modern conception of integrity of public servants in the sense that they should not use their official position to obtain any kind of financial or other advantage for themselves, their families or friends is due to the development of the rule of law and the evolution of a large, permanent public service. For the redressal of corrupt public servants Disciplinary Rules are available. The Prevention of Corruption Act, 1947 which has amended in 1988 provides ample power to the government for redressal of delinquent officials and their accomplices. The Supreme Court of India as well as the High Courts of States decided lots of corruption cases imposing penalties as per provisions of relevant sections and sub-sections of the Prevention of Corruption Act, 1947 and 1988. Prompt decisions of corruption cases in courts is an essential criteria for effective implementation of the provisions of the Act. Delay in taking decisions of such cases may be accounted as a limit of successful prosecution. There are also other limits causing failure in litigations. In analysing case laws we find some legislative requirement of sanction for prosecution. The case of R.S. Nayak- V- A.R. Antulay [14] may be taken as an example of such cases. For the offence under Sec. 11 of the Act, the essential ingredients, as observed by Honourable Justice Ranganath Misra in R.S. Nayak-V-A.R. Antulay are:

1. That the accused was a public servant.
2. That he accepted or obtained or agreed to accept or obtain a valuable thing without consideration or for an inadequate consideration knowing it to be inadequate.
3. That the person giving the thing must be a person concerned or interested in or related to the person concerned in any proceeding or business transacted or about to be transacted by the Government servant or having any connection with the official functions of himself or of any public, servant to whom he is subordinate and
4. The accused must have knowledge that the person giving the thing is so concerned or interested or related.

Under many circumstances, the existence of ingredients of the offence in question are difficult to prove in litigation. The procedural lapses of the prosecution as well as the delay in taking recourse creates complications in succeeding the prosecution. Special Judges and Magistrates have been notified for the trial of Special Police Establishment cases in all States excepting one in which such notifications are issued individually for each case. This causes delay in the finalisation of Charge -sheet and in the commencement of trials, Existing arrangement of entrusting responsibilities on the state government advocates to look after Special Police Establishment cases in the High Court is not proved satisfactory according to the findings of the Santhanam Committee on Prevention of Corruption.

Delay in conducting departmental or Disciplinary proceedings also caused a limitation in succeeding prosecution. These delays are undesirable from every point of view. The deterrent effect of punishment may be defeated due to such delay in prceeding. Procedural mistake and delay in taking actions in the departmental cases of corruption are the common features in Assam which is the major causes of defeating the objective of the Prevention of Corruption Act, 1947.

REFERENCES

1. Chandra, M. (1979), *Socio-Economic Crimes*, p. 60.
2. Govind, H. (1979), "Corruption: Causes and Cure," *Mainstream* (republic day issue; 1979).
3. Limaye, M. (1982), "How Grave is the Threat to the Nation," *Mainstream*; p. 21.
4. Chitta Ranjan, C.N. (1982), "Corruption Who is to Fight It?" *Mainstream*, May, 1982.
5. Kant, K. (1982), "Corruption And Electoral Process Mainstream," July 17, 1982.
6. Indrayan, N.K. (1985), *Law of Public Opinion on India*, p. 180.
7. Indrayan, N.K. (1985), *Law and Public Opinion In India*, p. 182.
8. High Denomination Bank Notes (Demonetisation) Act, 1978.
9. Balaji -V- I.T.O., 1962.2 S.C.R., 983 Followed in Umedray-V-C.I.T., 1965, A.P. 114.
10. Navanti Lal -V - I.T. Appellate Assistant Commissioner, 1965, A.S.C 1375.

11. *Committee On Prevention of Corruption* (1964), p. 110.
12. Paranjape, N.V. (1383), *Criminology and Penology*, p. 78.
13. Deb, R. (1982): *Principles of Criminology, Criminal Law and Investigation.*
14. R.S. Nayak -V- A.R. Antulay (1984); 2 Scc, 183.

4

Efficacy of the Prevention of Corruption Act 1947

Public Apathy

Unlike the traditional crimes, bribery and corruption does not carry any stigma with it and absence of any stigma enables this new category of criminals to move about in the society without any loss of status or respectability. The society or the community at large has meagre means to know and learn of the criminality of such persons, even the conviction and punishment of these upper class criminals is either not known to or not taken due notice of by the people. Publication of such conviction and punishment in newspapers is only casual in nature. It is necessary to give due and sufficient publicity in detail of those persons, firms and other organisations which have been convicted for corrupt practices. This publication will certainly create a climate against those offenders and it should be supplemented by a relatively more organised resentment by the community.

In the present day political setup the society is represented by the State. The relation between society and the crime is same as the relation between the State and crime. The State is meant to provide the individual, the protection which he could not expect to get otherwise than in a social organisation. A corrupt man is out for an easy gain at the expense of other persons and in whose good he is hardly interested.[1]

This is a matter of common knowledge that a number of penal statutes are not obeyed and enforced merely because they fail to keep time with the deep-rooted concepts in society, with the breaking of socially organised units into pieces, the members become more individualistic and self-centred and unconnected with social responsibilities which in turn results in increase crime rates.

Corruption and bribery continue to multiply partly because of their nature and partly because of the State's attitude of laissez faire and furthermore because of lack of any concerted effort and organised opposition by the society. Social consciousness is an important requirement to suppress anti-social activities in a society. Social consciousness against corrupt activities of a class of people may arouse through wide publicity to the convictions of persons for socio-economic crimes like corruption and bribery. Such publication would go a long way to degrade these criminals in the estimation and eyes of their fellow community beings, resulting in much improvement in the overall situation of socio-economic crimes. This may even in appropriate cases result in ex-communication of such criminals by their community and society. Publication may create a climate against corruption and it should be supplemented by a relatively more organised resentment by the community.

By today's standards it seems rather odd to argue that people who have the political power or highhanded protection to avoid prosecution are not criminals whatever may be the gravity of their offence. Political pressure is the most powerful weapon in its effort to corrupt the enforcement process. From the legislator's standpoint, regulatory agencies have two important advantages over the criminal justice system. For one thing, they make the law makers job easier by taking over the responsibility for the formation of specific rules, standards and guidelines. In the case of environmental pollution, for example, pollution must be identified, their effects on the public's health must be determined and a safe level of exposure must be set. In addition, numerous other issues concerning the specific techniques to be used to achieve these goals and the economic costs involved, must be decided. Although a legislative body could handle such questions, such a task would be extremely time consuming and would involve matters well beyond the expertise of most legislators. But the availability of such expertise is not the only advantage legislators have seen in the creation of regulatory agencies. Such agencies also provide a convenient place to pass the buck when politicians want to avoid making decisions that are likely to be unpopuler with an important constituency.[2]

Politics and bureaucracy must conform to meet the true social objectives of the nation. In our system, bureaucracy is a dirty word in the political lexicon and bureaucrats are the favourite whipping boys of the government and of Parliament when things seem to go wrong—and yet in a period of transition it is bureaucracy based on the concepts of permanence, independence, neutrality and anonymity which provides the element of consistency and continuity in a democratic framework, particularly in conditions of political anarchy and social chaos, it is the permanent services with which provide bellast for the ship of State[3] The overall achievement in respect of anti-corruption drive depends mainly upon the bureaucracies who are the guardians of law enforcement in the country. Existing laws for curbing corruption and malpractices are sufficient for the purpose. The only thing to be done is to enforce these laws rigidly. Nothing should be allowed to interfere while the law takes its course. By giving shelters to the corrupt people and anti-social elements, the parties in politics will try to continue to hoodwink the people whom they profess to serve. People at large have therefore to play a major role in the matter. They must be fearless, upright and ready to face any eventuality in upholding the ideal of honesty and truth, sufferings may increase in the process, but such sufferings will lay the foundations of a society free from corruption.[4] Time has come to launch such a campaign for eradicating corruption from public life, corruption in public life causes economic recession and economic recession geo-pardise personal insecurity in the society. People are suffering and feel themselves increasingly to be insecure in their accustomed life-style and expectations.

Corruption can exist only if there is someone willing to corrupt and capable of corrupting. Both this willingness and capacity to corrupt is found in a large measure in the industrial and commercial classes. Public participation in controlling corruption in the society is a dire need, Everyone in the society has duties to the community in which alone free and full development of his personality is possible.[5]

Non Implementation or Delay in Implementation of the Act

In the vast field of administrative action it *is* most likely that the procedures and practices in the working of government offices are cumbersome and time consuming. Similarly the procedures and practices to be followed in the process of implementation of the Prevention of Corruption Act, are in most of the cases radiculous in nature. Several procedures of the Act, directly or indirectly caused delay in investigation. Delay occasioned in securing the presence of official witnesses for examination. Unless the officials be made available for interrogation within a limited period, the objective of investigation may be defeated. In cases involving assets disproportionate to one's known sources of income, there is usually delay in obtaining from accounts Officers, statements regarding pay, allowances etc. of the government servants concerned. Delay in investigation also happened in cases where inquiries in foreign countries required. The process of obtaining reports from foreign countries is to depend on Indian Missions abroad. It cannot be a satisfactory arrangement in serious and complicated cases where quick investigation is an unavoidable need, moreover in many cases lacking in examination of all relevant points is the outcome of such enquiries, difficulties may also arise while expert opinion or technical assistance Is to obtain in a case. As it is *very* much difficult to achieve a satisfactory coordination amongst inter-departments, such opinion or technics! assistance which are to obtain from different agencies cause delay in investigation, Some other causes of delay in investigation and trial had enlightened in the Santhanam Committee Report on Prevention of Corruption such as delay in production of files of departmental inquiries to the Police Establishment for scrutiny, delay in conducting departmental proceedings etc. In most of the cases, the departmental or disciplinary proceedings against corrupt public servants takes lot of times and ultimately defeated the objective of the Act. These delays are undesirable from every point of view. They whittle down the deterrent effect of punishment. Examination of witnesses after a considerable lapse of time creates problem. Instances of pending departmental or disciplinary proceedings are innumerable. Such cases in the departments of the government are countless and inordinate deity in each CASES is a common phenomena. Several causes for such delay may be assessed on examination of departmental actions taken on such cases. Some of these causes are (1) lack of proper knowledge on the concerning rules and procedures of the dealing clerks as well as of the officer in authority. In the existing system of office procedures, the files are to put up by the concerning clerk with the actions to be taken by the authorised officer and the officer concern is to take decisions on the actions to be taken in a case and to process accordingly. In the process, due to ignorance of the procedures and the matters involved in the proposed action, the dealing clerk takes much time in placing the file to the officer. The officer who is to take decision, if dependable on the clerk in respect of the actions to be taken may create an additional problem of taking action timely. Under many circumstances, actions on the departmental or disciplinary proceedings seems to have taken in a wrong direction leaving a scope for the defendant to challenge the action in the court and ultimately the defendant —escapes inspite of consistent delinquency. Both non-action and delay in action in most of the departmental cases seems responsible for defeating the corruption cases. (2) creation of special favour by keeping close the disciplinary authority by faul means of the delinquent public servant. This is a type of corruption. The dealing clerk by using a delaying tactics keep the file pending for indefinite in period so as to suppress the case in taking any action at his own will in exchange of monetary benefit obtained from the corrupt public servant. Similar attitude also may be taken by the officer as disciplinary authority. (3) Highhandedness of the corrupt public servant is an another cause of failure in taking penal action against corruption. Political influence and interference of other persons in power also causes escape of corrupt public servants from any penalty to be imposed as per provision of the Act.

The investigating officer should see that there is no undue delay in recording statement for an unjustified period. Unexplained long delay on the part of the investigating officer in this matter will render evidence of such witnesses unreliable and cast a cloud of suspicion on the credibility of the entire or wrap and wool of the prosecution story. When statement of witnesses though examined on the date of occurrence were not reduced to writing until two days later it was held that, there evidence was of a tainted in nature and therefore could not be acted upon.[7]

If investigation and eventual trial of cases are delayed, the chances of miscarriage of justice and expenses of litigation increase tremendously. Delay gives an opportunity to the opposite party to win over witnesses and thus to vitiate the course of justice. It also results in loss of evidence for disinterested witnesses not being personally involved with the incident may often forget details of the occurrence after a certain lapse of time. Then again, many a time even the remedy provided by the law becomes infructuous due to efflux of time. Thus it is rightly said that "Justice delayed is justice denied."[8]

The new Criminal procedure Code of 1973 has emphasised the need for speedier investigation in criminal cases and in the case of petty offences has either barred investigation beyond a certain period of time or barred the taking of cognizance thereof by the court after a fixed time schedule.[9] The Supreme Court in a number of cases has severely condemned both prolong investigation and tardy administration of justice and held both to be evaluative of fundamental right guaranteed under Art. 21 of the Constitution. Thus where the period of limitation set by Sec. 456 of the new Code for filing a complaint or charge sheet had already expired the High Court either quashed the investigation,[10] or quashed the proceedings sending in court.[11] The High Courts and the Supreme Court have been quite concerned about the undue delay that every now and then comes to their notice in the disposal of cases and have often quashed long pending cases on ground of harassment to the accused. Indeed the High Courts and the Supreme Court have been quite concerned about the delay that every now and then concerned to their notice in the disposal of cases and have often quashed long pending cases on grounds of harassment to the accused. Thus in Prithi Raj's case[12] the Punjab and Haryana High Court quashed the pending case under sub-section 430/114/189 I.P.C. as in the opinion allowing the proceeding to continue after a period of eleven years was nothing but harassment to the accused, similarly in Kapil Das Sukala's cases[13] the Supreme Court quashed the case under sub-section 408/477 A I.P.C. as 20 years had already passed during which the accused had been kept in suspense. So also was the case of Uma Shankar[14] where the Supreme Court upheld the order of the Patna High Court quashing a charge under Sec. 7 of the Essential Commodities Act, 1955 as 20 years had already elapsed and the trial had not yet made much headway. It must however, be said in all fairness to the investigating officers, that at present their strength is inadequate and in addition to their duties as investigating officers, they are also saddled with all sorts of law and order, bandobest and V.I.P. duties which take a lot of their time to the detriment of investigation of cases[15] The Public Accounts Committees of States are examining the financial irregularities and misappropriation cases and in all the occasions it is a common feeling of the Committees that prompt action should be taken to penalise the officials for any irregularity. It has been the experience of the Public Accounts Committee that, at present little action is taken by the heads of departments when such cases come to their notice. Thus there being no fear or ewe of the authority, the irregularities are on the increase and more defects are creeping into the system.[16]

Delay in investigation and taking action against corrupt public servents at all levels at all times travelling from the high officials down to the lowest official responsible for estimating, spending and accounting causes corruption on the increase day by day. Delay in both internal and public inquiries have adverse effects in trapping corrupt public servants. The same problems more or less exists in all the countries of the world. The internal inquiries tend to be leaked asking the distinction a fairly academic one, but greater difficulty is experienced in trying to obtain the reports of internal inquiries.[17]

Procedural Lacunas in Trial and Investigation

Sec. 17 of the Prevention of Corruption Act, 1988 (Sec. 5-A (1) of The Prevention of Corruption Act, 1947) listed the persons authorised to investigate corruption cases. According to this section, no Police Officer below the rank

(a) in the case of the Delhi Special Police Establishment of an Inspector of Police;

(b) in the metropolitan areas of Bombay, Calcutta, Madras and Ahmedabad and in any other metropolitan areas notified as such under sub-section (1) of Sec. 8 of the Code of Criminal Procedure, 1973 of an Assistant Commissioner of Police;

(c) elsewhere of a Deputy Superintendent of Police or a Police officer of equivalent rank.

Shall investigate any offence punishable under this Act without the order of a Metropolitan Magistrate or a Magistrate of the first class, as the case may be, or make any arrest therefor without a warrant.

Provided that, if a Police officer not below the rank of an Inspector of Police is authorised by the State Government in this behalf by general or social order, he may also investigate any such offence without the order of a Metropolitan Magistrate or a Magistrate of the first class, as the case may be or make arrest therefor without a warrant:

Provided further that an offence referred to in clause (b) of sub-section (1) of Sec. 13 shall not be investigated without the order of a Police officer not below the rank of a Superintendent of Police.[18]

The Santhanam Committee on Prevention of Corruption assessed some lacunas in trial and investigation of corruption cases by anti-corruption agencies. Special provisions of procedures for certain categories of public servants without maintaining uniformity in such laws creates difficulty in discharging duties effectively. Requiring prior concurrence by the Special Police Establishment for starting inquiries or investigations against Railway Gazetted officers is a lacuna. There is no justification for such a condition. Although directives lay down that facilities should be offered to the Special Police Establishment by Ministries and Departments in obtaining official files and documents, such facilities have not seems provided causing delay and difficulties. The delaying act of producing official files and documents may provide scope to tamper or destroy materials. Similarly in some other existing procedures to be followed in investigation and trial of cases creates delay and inefficiency in the process. The same problems also being faced by the State Vigilance organisations. Communication of corruption cases to the vigilence establishment by the respective departments is much less only a few cases are being reported. The departmental actions to be taken after reporting are also carried on in a very irregular and slow process. Moreover, the staff of these vigilance organisations are not sufficient to work with the objective of the Prevention of Corruption Act, so promptly and efficiently. Such lacunas are to be removed for an efficient functioning of the anti-corruption organisations.

It has often been found that want of proper appreciation of the law of evidence and the ingredients of the offence, the investigating officers fail to collect the requisite evidence in course of the investigation and unwittingly keep loopholes through which the accused finds an easy way out of the grip of law.[19] Very often even the requisite evidence is not collected in accordance with the provisions of the procedures of the law and thereby making it difficult to use such evidence in a court of law. Thus only a sound knowledge of the ingredients of the substantive law and the rules of evidence and procedural law can enable an investigating officer to fully comprehend the requirements of the law for court purposes.[20] The Law Commission of India too felt that many trials are defeated in court, because most of our investigating officers, not being law graduates and not having sufficient knowledge of law and court procedure, fail to understand if a particular piece of evidence is important to the prosecution, whether any links in the chain of circumstantial evidence are missing, whether any connected subject requires to be investigated in order to fill up lacunas in the prosecution case and such other related matters.[21] In many advanced countries, a good deal of emphasis is given on the legal qualification of the candidates at the time of recruitment to the investigating branch of the Police.[22] If a lawyer can know what to keep from a jury, a lawyer should also know what to get before a jury.[23] Lack of legal knowledge of an investigating officer resulted in spoiling good many cases.

Under the existing provisions of staff and other facilities of various anti-corruption establishments, a wide coordinated action of other connected departments are needed. A vast experience of inquiring corruption cases by vigilance and other anti-corruption departments indicates that, such a coordination is difficult to achieve to the desired extent. The paradoxical achievement is due to various reasons. So, all the specialised staff if under the control of the head of the anti-corruption organisation, then perhaps a better coordination of all such specialised personnel be possible.

Trial follows cognizance and cognizance is preceded by investigation. This is undoubtedly the basic scheme of the code in respect of cognizable cases. But, only a limited cases proceed on to the trial stage due to failure in prior levels.

Another major lacuna of the Prevention of Corruption Act, is that the Act and the provisions of the I.P.C. and conduct rules does not cover the MLA's, MPs who may practise corruption with free hand. This inconsistency of the Act appeared in the litigation of the case of R.S. Nayak- V - A.R. Antulay. Where offences as set out in Sec. 6 of the I.P.C. are alleged to have been committed by a public servant, sanction of only that authority would be necessary who would be entitled to remove him from that which is alleged to have been misused or abused for corrupt motives. MLA is not comprehended in clause seventh of Sec. 21 so as to be a public servant.

Non-Relief of Prosecution Cases at Appellate Level

Offences of bribery and corruption have now the subject matter of a special branch of criminal law. For the investigation and trial of these offences, the special provisions of the Prevention of Corruption Act, 1947 and the Criminal Law Amendment Act, 1952 have to be applied in preference to the general law. Offences of accepting or obtaining any illegal gratification or accepting or obtaining any valuable thing without consideration by a public servant and the abetment of these offences are dealt with by Sec. 161, 165-A of the I.P.C. In addition to these provisions, a special offence of criminal misconduct by a public servant has been created under Sec. 5 of the Prevention of Corruption Act. Failure of prosecution cases at appealate level arises due to inconsistencies in framing up and in any stage of their investigation and trial as per provisions indicated above, where the order made by a Civil Court appointing a Commissioner for seizing the books of the plaintiff is null and void as being without jurisdiction under the Civil Procedure Code, the person so appointed is not a public servant and even when a bribe is offered to him, the offering of the bribe is not an offence under Sec. 165-A of the Penal Code. In Daulat Ram -V- State of Punjab, assumption of cognizance by the Magistrate, of an offence under Sec. 182 of the Penal Code on such a chargesheet filed by the police, without the complaint in writing of the public servant concerned is wrong and incompetent, and the trial being without jurisdiction ab initio, conviction cannot be maintained.[24] In Padam Sen -V- State of Uttar Pradesh[25] the accused was charged under Sec. 165-A Penal Code for having offered a bribe to the respondent, a person appointed by a Civil Court as Commissioner in a suit under Sec. 75 and Order 26 of the Code of Civil Procedure. The Commissioner was appointed for seizing the account books of the plaintiff, In this prosecution case, the trial court convicted the accused and on appeal, the High Court confirmed the conviction. On appeal, the Supreme Court allowed and order of conviction made against the appellant was set aside, he was acquitted of the offence under Sec. 165-A. It was held in this case that, Sec. 75 of the Code empowers a civil court to issue a commission only for the four purposes set out in the section. A commission cannot be issued for any other purpose under Sec. 75. Therefore the Civil Court had no power to appoint a commissioner for seizing the books of account of the plaintiff and the order appointing the respondent as Commissioner was therefore null and void. The second contention was that Explanation 2 to Sec. 21 of the Penal Code provides that the word " public servant" as used in the section covers "every person who is in actual possession of the situation of a public servant, whatever legal defect there might be in his right to hold that situation". In the present case, there was no existing office of Commissioner, nor had the Munsiff any power to appoint the Respondent as commissioner for the purpose of seizing the plaintiff's accounts books. It must therefore be held that the Explanation did not apply to the appointment of the Respondent as commissioner, and as his appointment was null and void, he was not a public servant within the meaning of Sec. 21, Clause 4 of the Penal code. Since the respondent was not a public servant at the time when the bribe was offered to him, the offence under See. 165-A was not committed by offering him money.

Many cases at appellate level fails due to absence of certain relevant and accurate assessment procedures of properties disproportionate to the known sources of income. According to Sec. 5 (1) (e) of the Prevention of corruption Act, 1947, a public servant is said to commit the offence of criminal misconduct if he or any person on his behalf is in possession or has at any time during the period of his office, been in possession for which the public servant cannot satisfactorily accounts of pecuniary resources or property disproportionate to his known sources of income. In order to establish that a public servant is in possession of pecuniary resources and property. Disproportionate to his known sources of income, it is not imperative that the period of reckoning be spread out for the entire stretch of anterior service of the public servant. There can be no general rule or criterion, valid for all cases, in regard to their choice of the period for which accounts are taken to establish criminals misconduct under Sec. 5 (1) (e). The choice of the period must necessarily be determined by the allegations of fact on which the prosecution is founded and rests. However, the period must be such as to enable a true and comprehensive picture of the known sources of income and the pecuniary resources and property in possession of the public servant either by himself or through any other person on his behalf, which are alleged to be so disproportionate. In State of Maharashtra- (Appellant) -V- Pollonji Darabshaw Daruwalls (Respondent)"[26], the appeal failed on the contention that, the High Court was in error in holding that a public servant charged for having disproportionate assets in his possession for which he cannot satisfactorily account cannot be convicted of an offence under Sec. 5 (2) read with Sec. 5 (1) (e) of the Act. Unless the prosecution disproves all possible sources of income. The respondent must be given the benefit of doubt. Similarly in Bal Krishna Sayal (Appellant) -V- State of Punjab (Respondent)[27] the prosecution has failed to establish its case beyond reasonable doubt and the appellant is entitled to this benefit of this situation. As such the appeai prosecution has failed at appelate level.

To establish an illegal gratification the prosecution must prove the nexus between the illegal gratification and the official act. Otherwise it will fail on that ground. Negligence on the part of the prosecution also may cause failure in leading the evidence in connection with the official act.[28]

In most of the cases, the causes of failure of prosecution at appealate level may be attributed as:

1. negligence on the part of the disciplinary authority.
2. negligence on the part of the prosecuting authority.
3. inefficiency of the authorities arising out of lacking knowledge in relevant discipline and thereby fail to establish the charges,
4. suppression of facts in investigation in consideration of bribes.

A charge under Sec. 7-A of the Prevention of Corruption Act, 1947 (new Section 22) is one which is easily and may often be lightly, made but, in the very nature of things difficult to establish, as direct evidence must, in most cases, be meagre and of a tainted nature. Those considerations, however, cannot be suffered to relieve the prosecution of any part of the burden which rests upon it to establish the charts beyond reasonable doubt. If after everything that can legitimately be considered has been given its due weight, room still exists for taking the view that however strong the suspicion raised against the accused, every reasonable possibility of innocence has not been excluded, he is entitled to an acquittal.[29] In case of the accused satisfactorily accounted for acquisition of assets, charge under Sec. 5 (2) cannot be sustained and in that case the prosecution will fail. The charge against the appellant was that, curing a certain period he committed criminal misconduct in the discharge of his duties as a public servant and obtained pecuniary advantage for himself and others by giving contractors favourable rates in respect of earth work done by them and by acquisition of assets worth more than Rupees three lakhs which were disproportionate to his known sources of income and thereby committed an offence punishable under Sec. 5 (2) and with Sec. 5 (1) (a) to 5 (l) (d) of The Prevention of Corruption Act, 1947. The Supreme Court upon a review of the evidence as a whole found that the appellant-has satisfactorily accounted for the acquisition of his assets to the extent of Rupees three lakhs. It was therefore held that the presumption under Sec. 5 (3) which has since been amended cannot be applied. It was further held that in the absence of presumption arising under Sec. 5 (0) of the Act, the conviction of the appellant for the charge under Sec. 5 (2) of the Act, cannot be sustained.[30]

Sometimes the prosecution against corrupt public servant failed at appellate level due to non -fulfilment of essential conditions as per provision of the relevant section. When the provisions of Sec. 6 are examined, it is manifest that two conditions must be fulfilled before its provisions become applicable. One is that the offence mentioned therein must be committed by a public servant and the other is that, person is employed in connection with the affairs of the Union or a State and is not removable from his office save by or with the sanction of the Central government or the state government or is a public servant who is removable from his office by any other competent authority. Both these conditions must be present to prevent a court from taking cognizance of an offence mentioned in the section without the previous sanction of the Central government or the State government or the authority competent to remove the public servant from his office. If either of these conditions is lacking, the essential requirements of the section are wanting and the provisions of the section do not stand in the way of a court taking cognizance without a previous sanction. On the plea of lacking essential conditions, the prosecution in S.A. Venkataraman -V- The State[31] failed at appellate level. The provisions of the section 6 of the Prevention of Corruption Act, is not applicable when the accused is not charged under Sec. 161 or Sec. 165 of the I.P.C. or under sub-section (2) or subsection (3-A) of section 5 of The Prevention of Corruption Act, but under certain other section of the Penal Code, Under such circumstances, the prosecutions in Bhup Narain Sexena -V- State[32] Om Prakash- V - State[33], State -V- Pandurang Buberao.[34] Amrendra Nath Roy -V- State[35], and Ganga Serein - V -State[36] failed at appellate level. The law of sanction be invariably implemented irrespective of the nature of offence of corruption. It cannot be evaded by referring to an offence which does not require sanction. In K.P, Sinha -V - Aftabuddin[37] Osman Mistry -V- Atul Krishna,[38] Bas-Ul-Huq -V- State of West Benga[39] and N. Brahmeswararao -V- Sub-Inspector of Police, the question which required answer was whether the law of sanction could be avoided by referring to an offence which did not require sanction although the facts disclosed also an offence which require sanction. Held that the law of sanction for prosecution under Sec. 161 or for an offence under Sec. 5 (1) (d) of The Prevention of Corruption Act, as provided by Sec. 6 of The Prevention of Corruption Act, cannot be evaded. When the facts of corruption cases upon which accused is to be prosecuted did not consider by the sanctioning authority, the prosecution must fail at the appellate level. In Mohd. Iqbal Ahmed -V- State of A.P.[40], conviction and sentences passed on the appellant were quashed.

Grant of sanction by others other than competent authority also vitiates prosecution. Competency of authority to grant sanction to be proved by rules. In V.V. Joshi -V- State[41] the accused, a class III Railway employee was appointed by

Divisional Personnel officer. Sanction for prosecution was granted by Divisional Medical officer, divisional Medical Officer and Divisional Personnel-Officer are officers of equal rank, Divisional Personnel Officer made the appointment as an officer who had been delegated with the powers of a General Manager. Nothing to show that powers of General Manager in this respect were delegated to Divisional Medical Officer, divisional Medical Officer not being competent to remove the accused, the sanction granted by him was invalid. As such conviction of the accused set aside. In Republic of India -V- Khagendra Nath[43], the prosecution of the accused failed at appellate level due to incompetency to sanction accorded by lower authority. In this case, the Executive Committee of the Central Board of State Bank of India who is the authority to appoint and dismiss officers of all categories of the State Bank of India did not accord sanction of prosecution. The Local Board who has no such power, accorded sanction, sanction for prosecution for offences under Prevention of Corruption Act, had to be accorded by Executive Committee. Nothing to show that Local Board is in any way authorised under the Act of Regulations to accord sanction or to dismiss an officer. Sanction order by Local Board cannot be said to be valid in the eye of law. It was held that, in the absence of proper sanction the prosecution becomes illegal.

It is for the prosecution to show that valid sanction given by the authority authorised to give it under Sec. 6 (1) of the Act, and such authority is no doubt the authority competent to remove the employee in question from his office and by virtue of Article 311 of the Constitution of India and Rule 1705 of the Railway Establishment Code. Volume 1, such an authority was the authority who had appointed the employee to the post held by him substantively. It is for the prosecution to show that valid sanction had been given. On the ground of invalid sanction accorded in Makhan Lal -V- State,[44] Matajong Dobey -V- H.C. Bhari,[45] Madan Mohan Singh -v-

State of U.P.,[46] Mohanlal Keshavlal -v- State[47] and Rampukar Singh -v- State,[49] the convictions of accused parson set aside. In Bhuneswar Prasad -v- State of Bihar[49] and Ram Pukar Singh -V- State[50] no sanction order was duly proved. As such the entire prosecution of the appellant failed for want of a duly proved sanction order as required by law.

When an essential part of the prosecution case has disbelieved in which the other part was dependent, the prosecution is to fail. In Hari Dev Sharma- V - State, the nigh Court disbelieved the pert of the prosecution case which has the genesis of the case. The prosecution case was one integrated story. It was held on evidence that -

(a) if the High Court did not accept a vital part of the story, the other part did not stand by itself and could not be accepted.

(b) It was not the prosecution case that the money which was recovered from the appellant, was the amount that the appellant had asked for from the complainant. This was a new ease made by the High Court.

(c) The High Court having disbelieved a part of the prosecution case on which the other part was dependent, it is not safe to sustain the conviction of the Appellant.

Similarly in Loknath Dash -V- State of Orissa[52], the prosecution has failed and the conviction of the appellant set aside. Sometimes the prosecution fails due to unreliable substantive evidence. In Suraj Mal - V -State,[53] Kailash Chandra Babu -V- State of Orissa[54] and Ram Kishore -V- state[55], it was held that, mere recovery of money divorced from the circumstances under which it is paid is not sufficient to convict the accused when the substantive evidence in the case is not reliable.

When a prosecution failed to prove the guilt of taking bribe by the accused, the prosecution fails at appellate level, where the accused, an Engineer was convicted by the special Judge under Sec. 13 (l) (d) (Old Sec. 5 (l) (d)) read with Sec. 13 (2) (old Sec. 5 (2) and Sec 7 (old Sec. 161 I.P.C.) and the conviction was upheld by the High Court, Honourable Supreme Court set aside the conviction as the prosecution failed to prove the guilt of the accused. It was observed that the foundation of the prosecution case of the demand made by the accused for bribe has been shaken to a grant extent. It has cast a grave doubt on the subsequent event that was alleged to have taken place in the matter of giving of bribe to the accused and the recovery of bribe money from him coupled with the unusual behaviour of the contractor in purchasing sweets and fruits for the accused. The accused was found to be honest and his service record showed that he was an officer of integrity throughout his career, He has no movable or immovable property. For the defence of the case he has borrowed rupees six thousand from his G.P.F. account. The accused was acquitted.[56]

In Amrit Lal -V - State of Punjab[57]

(a) the evidence about the demand for illegal gratification having been made comprised of the solitary statement of an interested witness.

(b) there was then no evidence about any talk between the giver and the receiver that the money changed hands as a bribe.

(c) the appellant had been able to produce two subordinates from his office who said that the money had remained lying on the table and had never been put in his pocket by the appellant.

(d) the defence evidence found support from the official records which did not appear to be fabrication.

It WAS held that under the circumstances the case would not be described to be quite free from doubt, and the appellant's conviction and sentence were therefore, liable to be set aside.

In Jai Ram Lakhe - V - State of Punjab[58] the appellant is acquitted, as the facts are sufficient to raise a serious doubt about the guilt of the appellant.

It was held in this case that -

(a) The trial court and the High Court have not taken the relevant facts and circumstances into consideration even though they have been established by the evidence on record and have a direct bearing on the guilt of the appellant.

(b) the currency notes were recovered from one S and not from the possession of the appellant. There was no evidence to show that there were any visible marks by which could show that they had been handled by the appellant. These facts are sufficient to raise a serious doubt about the guilt of the appellant.

In the case of Kanchan Singh Dholak Singh Thakur -V- State of Gujarat [59], the conviction of the appellant under Sec. 5 (2) of the Prevention of Corruption Act, (New Sec. 13) was based mainly on Entry A-18 from which it appeared that the appellant that misappropriated a sum of Rs. 1750/. It was also alleged that the appellant forged the signature of R on various dates to show payment of Rs. 2.50 although these payments were not made to at all. The entire conviction rested on the uncorroborated testimony of an expert (P.W.). The High Court found that the expert had opined that in case of even those persona who admitted to have signed in token of the payment, the signatures of the witnesses were forged. It was held by the Supreme Court that -

(a) At any rate, the expert's opinion is not reliable. Once

it is proved that the appellant had not forced hie signature on the Entry, there is no legal evidence to prove, - (i) the charge of misappropriation or (ii) use of forced document or (iii) the charge of corruption or (iv) the allegation of forgery.

(b) It is well settled that, in order to rely on the evidence of an expert, the court must be fully satisfied that he is a truthful witness and also a reliable witness fully adept in the art of identification of handwriting in order to opine whether the alleged handwriting has been made by a particular person or not.

(c) As the evidence of the expert has been disbelieved by the High Court on the most material points, it is most unsafe to base the conviction of the appellant merely on the testimony of the expert.

(d) Apart from that, the possibility that the signature in the Entry might have been forged by one of the other officers and not the accused, has not been excluded by the prosecution.

(e) Therefore the prosecution has not proved beyond reasonable doubt in the result, the conviction passed on the appellant is set aside and he is acquitted of the charges framed against him.

In case of Prem Kumar -v- State of Punjab[60] the appellant's conviction under Sec. 5 (2) of the Act (New Sec. 13) is set aside due to absence of an independent corroboration of the evidence.

Section 20 (1) (old section 4 (1)) requires presumption of guilt of accused to be raised whenever it is shown that accused person has accepted any gratification other than legal remuneration or any valuable thing. In case of failure to prove the presumption, the prosecution will fail ultimately at the appellate level, The scope and extent of this presumption has been expounded in the Cases of Moolraj -V- State[61] Mehar Singh Hajara Singh - V -State[62], State -V- Minaketan Patnaik[63], Mitra - V -State[64], Krishnabiherilal -V- State[65], Narayan - V - State[66], Lalchand Topindae -V- State[67], Ranjit Singh - V - State,[68] State -V- Abhey Singh,[69] Akhouri Inder-deo Prasad - V- state[70].

It was held that -

(a) The initial burden of proving that the accused accepted or obtained the amount other than legal remuneration, is upon the prosecution.

(b) It is only when this initial burden is successfully discharged by the prosecution that the burden of proving the defence shifts upon the accused and a presumption would arise under Sec 20 (l) (old Sec. 4 (1)) of the Act.

(c) The accused would have to discharge this burden by disproving that he accepted or obtained the amount as gratification other than legal remuneration.

(d) therefore the prosecution evidence is first required to be seen by the Special Judge.

(e) The prosecution has failed to discharge the initial burden of proving that the money was accepted or obtained by the appellant is gratification other then legal remuneration.

The prosecution evidence is certainly required to be assessed beyond the realm of reasonable doubt for discharging the initial burden that lies upon the prosecution, and if such evidence is not forthcoming, the appellant would be given the benefit of the same.

Therefore, the presumption under Sec. 20 (1) (old Sec. 4 (1) of the act, did not arise at all.[71]

In absence of legal sanction for prosecution, the condition precedent for taking cognizance of a case is absent. On this ground, failure of prosecution at appellate level may arise. In Nirmelendu Biswas -V- State (Through the Delhi Special Police Establishment)[72] it was held by the Gauhati High Court, that in view of issuing sanction for prosecution without authority, the Doctrine of De-facto will not be applicable in respect of the sanction order, and as such the condition precedent for taking cognizance of this case by the trial court was absent. On this ground alone the trial and the impunged judgement and order are liable to be quashed.

Political Interference

Records on criminal justice and enforcement of law confirmed that the criminal activities of the elite receive only token punishment. Though the Constitution of India under Article 14 guaranteed to all the citizens (1) equality before the law and (2) equal protection of law, it seems extremely difficult to treat the crimes of the privileged and the crimes of the powerless equally. The overall picture is a complex one and a more detailed analysis is necessary.

In the context of political interference one has to take into account the undue pressure that is sometimes put on the Executive Magistracy on the police or the prosecution to do or not to do certain things either during a state of unrest or at the stage of the investigation, or during the pendency of the proceedings, before the courts.[73] The discretion to take disciplinary or legal action against a delinquent is given to the police or other officers under the law and not to any political boss or other extraneous agency. So, any direction to the Police or other officials beyond the law by an extraneous agency, including the political Executive will, apart from demoralising the officials, be clearly illegal and malafide.[74] Law does not make any distinction between a superior or subordinate in this regard, irrespective of high or low official position, an officer is squarely held responsible for his illegal actions and neither an order of the superior nor ignorance of law, is an excuse under Sec. 76 or 79 of the Indian Penal Code. Since an officer is an agent of the law and also does not get protection of the law for carrying out an illegal order, it is he and he alone as has been sain by Geoffrey Marshall, what should be left free to decide as to whether he would or would not carry out the illegal order. It would be highly unjust to deny him this bare freedom when in the long run it is he who has to face the music 97 before the bar of justice. To disobey illegal orders of superior authority whether he be a political boss or an official superior, one must have a moral courage of high order and an indomitable will to uphold the Rule of Law.

Political pressure is the elite's most powerful weapon in its effort to corrupt the enforcement process. There is substantial question as to where to place criminal justice workers in this paradigm of influence and power. This issue can be resolved only in relation to specific objectives, workers such as policemen in vigilance organisations, attorneys, Public defenders and administrators may be seen as both victimizers and victims. They are victimizers in the sense that they directly administer the systems inequitable and unjust practices. The interplay between politics and the police often focusses exclusively upon the external influences and controls that are illegal and improper.[76]

Integrity of Officials in Trapping or Initiating Proceeding Against Delinquents

The investigation officer is not prohibited from laying trap in investigation. He may lay trap with decoy. By laying such trap, he cannot be said to have instigated or promoted the commission of the offence. He may submit report under Sec. 173, Cr.P.C. both in respect of offence informed and of offence committed during investigation and such course cannot be held illegal."

Success at Bureaucratic Desk

Using public office for private gain is a criminal process of injury to the public interest. The criminal Codes emphasise *the* breach of law, the consequences are only additional considerations, not primary. Corruption may be defined as the acquisition of forbidden benefits by officials or employees, so bringing into question their loyalty to their employer. Study of corruption, its causes and consequences suggests that three principal factors are involved in this white collar crime. These are the salaries paid, the opportunities presented for illegal use of office and policing to mean both direction and punishment. Corruption should not be thought to be dependent only on the level of salaries, or the efficiency of policing system or the opportunities present, but on ell three together. Corruption will be most prevalent when salaries are low, opportunities great and policing weak. It will be infrequent when the reverse applies, and salaries are generous, opportunities few and policing strong. So, the success at the bureaucratic desk in curbing corruption depends on the standard of ethical behaviour of officials and other authorities and creation of an atmosphere to suppress these criminalities.

Though India has the longest history of anti-corruption work, the problem of corruption continue to carry in endemic nature. All the anti-corruption departments and agencies both of the Central Government as well as of State governments have been reasonably effective in controlling corruption at certain levels. On the other hand, though corruption may have been contained, it has not been reduced even to a small extent. The weakness of policing and degradation of morality amongst administrators are the main reasons of this state of affairs. Along with removing the weaknesses of policing, a strict adherence to a high standard of ethical behaviour is required to eradicate the problem from public life. Anti-corruption work requires more then just investigation and prosecution.

REFERENCES

1. Quadri, S.M.A. (1982), *Crime, Society and Law.*
2. Coleman J.W. (1987), *The Criminal Elite: The Sociology of White Collar Crime*, p. 155.
3. Shahabuddin, 3. (1982), Toning up The Bureaucracy; *Mainstream*; Annual Issue.
4. Sen, 3. (1979): Time to Fight Corruption; *Mainstream*, March 3, p. 23.
5. Deb, R. (1968), *Police and Law Enforcement*; p. 55.
6. Balakrishna -V- State of Orissa, 1971, Cr. L.J 670 (SC); Krishan Lal -V- State, 1971; C.R. L.J. 1610 (Del); G.B. Patel -V- State of Maharashtra, 1979; C.R. L.J 51. (SC Pare 29): Banwari -V- State of Rajasthan, 1979, CR. L.J 161 (Raj.) Haradhan -V-State of A.P., 1981 CR.L.J. NOC 158 (Cal).
7. Ginduchi Patnaik -V- State of Orissa, 1985; Cr.L.J. 645 (Orissa).
8. Deb, R. (1988): Police And Law Enforcement, p. 166.
9. Nimeon Sangma -V - Govt. of Meghalya, 1979; Cr.L.J. 941 (SC) and Hussainara Khatoon -V- State of Bihar, 1973; Cr.L.J 1036 (SC) 1979 Cr.L.J. 1045 (SC) and 1979 Cr.L.J. 1052 (SC)
10. Balgopal Goenka -V- State of W.B., 1983 Cr. L.J. 570 (Cal.).
11. Wasata -V- State of Maharashtra; 1984 Cr. L.J. 410 (Bom).
12. Prithi Raj-V- State of Haryana, 1981; Cr. L.J. 948 (P &H)
13. State of U.P - V -Kapil Deo Shukla, 1972. Cr.L.J 1214 (SC)
14. State of Bihar -V - Uma Shankar, 1981; Cr. L.J. 159 (SC).
15. Sharma, Dr. Shankar Dayal (1985): Sardar Vellabh Bhai Patel Memorial Lecture- IT on "Rule of Law and Role of Police", S.V.P. National Academy, Hyderabad; p. 14.
16. Public Accounts Committee (1953): Audit Report, Assam.
17. Rele Stephen (1983): The Land of Waving Palms; Political Economy, Corruption Inquiries and Politics in sierra Leone; Corruption.
18. Swaroop, V. (1990), Prevention of Corruption Act, 1988; p. 336.
19. Deb, B. (1988), Police and Law Enforcement Ch. 14, p. 130.

20. Deb, R. (1990): Principles of Criminology, Criminal Law and Investigation; Vol. II, pp. 395-396.
21. Law Commission of India, 14th Report, Vol. II, pp. 736, 742 (1958).
22. Kanetkar, I.P.G.V. (1959): Visit to Europe; Bombay Police Journal, vol. X, No. 1, Jan., 1959; p. 4 (6).
23. Cooper, R. (1935); Ten Thousand Public Enemies' Blue Ribbon Books.
24. Daulat Ram -V- State of Punjab (1962): AIR 1206
25. padam Sen -V- State of Uttar Pradesh (1961); A.I.R, (S.C.), 218; S.C.R. 884; Cr.L.J 322.
26. State of Maharashtra -V- Pollonji Darabshaw Daruwalla (1988); A.I.R. 1988; S.C. 88.
27. Bal Krishna Sayal -V- state of Punjab (1987); S.C. 689 (From Punjab and Haryana).
28. Tare Prasad Banerjee -V- State of Bihar, 1973, Patna, L.J.P. 530.
29. H.T. Huntley -V- Emperor (1944), A.I.R. F.C. 66; 45, Cr.L.J. 755; 214 199; 1944 FLJ 167.
30. B.R. Subbatyya -V- State of Bihar (1970); I.S.C.W.R., 592, 1370; Current Law Journal, 457.
31. S.A. Venkataraman -V- The State,. A.I.R., 1958; S.C. 107,1958. S.C.J. 594,1958; S.C.R. 1037.
32. Bhup Narain Saxena -V- State; A.I.R. 1952. Allahabad 35.
33. Om Prakash -V- State; A.I.R. 1955, Allahabad 275.
34. State -V- Pandurang Bubarao, A.I.R. 1955; Bombay 450.
35. Amarender Nath Roy -V- State; A.I.R. 1955; Calcutta 236.
36. Ganga Karain -V- State, A.I.R. 1956; Allahabad 197.
37. K.P. Sinha -V- Aftabuddin, A.I.R. 1955; Patna 453.
38. Osman Mistry -V- Atul Krishna, A.I.R., 1949. Calcutta 632.
39. Bas-Ul-Haq -V- State U-Huq of west Bengal, A.I.R.. 1953; S.C. 293,1953; S.C.R. 836, 1953, Cr.L.J;., 1232, 1953; S.C.J. 405.
40. K. Brahmeswarao -V- Sub-Inspector of Police, Vimkanda, 1978; Cr.L.J. 1005 (A.P.).
41. Mohd. Iqbal Ahmed -V- State of, A.P. A.I.R 1979, S.C. 677, 197-3 Cr.L.J. 633,1379; A.C.C. 132.
42. V.V. Joshi -V- State; A.I.R. 1368; Punjab 120.
43. Republic of India -V- Khagendra Nath, 1982; Cr.L.J. 361 (orissa)
44. Makhan Lal -v- State; A.I.R. 1959, Rajasthan 214.

45. Matajong Dobey -V- H.C. Bhari; A.I.R. 1956, S.C. 44.
46. Madan Mohan Singh -V- State of U.P.; A.I.R. 1954, S.C. 637.
47. Mohanlal Keshavlal -v- State; A.I.R. 1956, Bombay 504.
48. Rampukar Singh -V- State, 1381; Cr.L.J. 1631.
49. Bhuneswar Prasad Singh -V- State of Bihar, 1981; Cr.L.J. 142.
50. Ram Pukar Singh - V- State, A.I.R. 1954; All. 234, 1954; Cr.L.J. 459.
51. Hari Dev Sharma -V- State; A.I.R. 1976, S.C. 1489 (1976) 1 Sev. I.C. 246; 1976 Cr.App.R. (S.C.) 201; 1376 L.J. (S.C.) 802; 1976 Cr.L.J. 1176; 1976 Cr.L.R. (S.C.) 264; (1976) 2 S.C.W.R. 26 (2 Judges) overruling 1971 Cr.L.J. 1615 (Delhi).
52. Loknath Dash -V- State of Orissa, 1977; Cr.L.J. 1268; 1977 Cut.L.R. (Cri.88) 1977, 43 Cut.L.T. 478 (Cri.)S.T.
53. Suraj Mal - V - State (Delhi Administration); A.I.R. 1979 S.C. 1408; 1980 (Mad. L.J. (Cri.) 73; (1979) 2 S.C.J. 516; 1979 Cr.L.R. (SC) *717*; 1979 (Cr.L.J. 1087); 1979 Cur L.J. (Cr) 155; 1979 U.J. (SC) 916; 1979 S.C. Cr.R. 313.
54. Kailash Chandra Babu -V- State of Orissa, 1988 (2) Crimes 609.
55. Ram Kishore -V- State (1987) 31 D.T. 312.
56. G.V. Nan Judiah -V- State (Delhi Administrations) A.I.R. 1987, S.C. 2402; 1988, Cr.L.J. 152; (1907) 3 Crimes 217; (1987) 33 DLT 96; 1387 S.C. Cr.R. 303; *(1987) 2 S*erv-L.J. 244; 1987 Cr.L.R. (SC) 580; (1987) 2 Supreme 345; (1987) Cal. Cr. L.R. (SC) 189 1987 All. Cr.C. 450; (1987) 3 IJ. Rep. 559 (1987) 4 J.T. 313; (1987) 23 Tax Law Rev. 1.
57. Amrit Lal -V- State of Punjab: 1972 CLR 210 1973, Cur.I..J. 260.
58. Jai Ram Lakhe -V- State of Punjab (1978)9 SCC 1978 Cr.L.R. 180; 1978 UJ (SC) 266; (1978) 2 SCWR 104, 1978 SCC (Cr) 357;1978 SC Cr.R.235.
59. Kanchan Singh Dholak Singh Thakur -V- State of Gujarat; A.I.R. 1979, S.C. 1011 (2 Judges); (1979)4 SCC 599; 1977 Mad. L.J. (Cr) 589; (1979) SCJ 260; (1973) UJ (SC) 551;1373 Cur.L.J. (Cr) 216; 1979 Cr.L.J. 889; 1976 Cr.L.R. (SC) 246.
60. Prem Kumar -V- State of Punjab (1978); CLR 366 (Punjab)
61. Moolraj -V- State (1955), Cr.L.J. 1585; A.I.R. 1955, Him.Pra. 57.
62. Mehar Singh Hajara Singh -v- State (1955), Cr.L.J. 1387; A.I.R. 1955, Pepsu 156.
63. State -V- Minaketan Patnaik (1952) Cr.L.J. 139; A.I.R. 1952, Orissa 267.

64. Kitra -V- State; A.I.R. 1951, Cal. 524.
65. Krishnabiharilal -V- State (1956) Cr.L.J. 232 (2) A.I.R. 1956, Madh. B 36.
66. Narayan -v- State (1956) Cr.L.J. 227; A.I.R. 1956. Madh. B 51.
67. Lalchand Topindas -V- State, A.I.R. 1956; Orissa 201; ILR 1956, Cut. 517, 22 Cut. LT 397;1956 Cr.L.J. 341.
68. Ranjit Singh -V- State (1957) Cr.L.J. 42 (All.) 1956 ALJ. 662.
69. State -v- Abhey Singh (1957) Cr.L.J. 541; A.I.R. 1957, Raj, 108; 1958 Ker. 136.
70. Akhouri Inderdeo Prasad -V- State;. A.I.R. 1958, pet. 374.
71. Khembu Ram -V- State, 1972, Cr. L.J. 381 Haim. Pra. 1371 Sim. L.J. (H.P) 283.
72. Sri Narmalendu Biswas -V- State (through the Delhi Special Police establishment) 1987) 2 GLR (NCC)5.
73. Deb, R. (1988), *Police and law Enforcement*, p. 111.
74. Deb, R. (1978), "Public Services Under the Rule of Law - Risht to Disobey illegal Orders," Journal of the Indian Law Institute, Oct. to Dec. 1978, p. 574.
75. Deb, R. (1980), "Public Service under the rule of Law", *Indian Police Journal,* Ministry of Home Affairs; Govt. of India; Jan. to March, p. 43.
76. Charles R. Swanson and Leonard Territo (1983), *Police Administration,* p. 23.
77. Chockalingam, in re 1969, Mad. I.W. (Cr.) 90.

5

Effect of Prosecution on Quality of Public Life

Corruption has maligned public life to a saturation point to day. It has entered every walk of life, To speak the truth law almost never touches the big man, the important public figure responsible for the destiny of the nation. It is common in many developing states to advocate severe measures in order to control corruption. Japan, during the Tokugawn period practised branding, cutting the hand that played the mischief, and similar corporal punishment. In Soviet Russia, punishment for crimes against the State has been the severest.[1] Like other countries of the world India also has been facing an unprecedented situation arising out of unabated growth of corruption. The aberrations of bribery and corruption are born of greed, avarice and rapaciousness and are a peculiar feature of persons of respectability and high social status in an acquisitive and affluent society and they all affect not only the health and material welfare of the individual, but also the economic structure and social fabric of a nation.

It is easy to criticise and condemn corruption, but it is difficult to eliminate it from human society, and much more difficult to avoid being tempted into it when our own turn comes. Prosecution of corrupt people cannot change the main Stream of this evil in the society. Root, out of corruption from public life needs to achieve high standard of ethical behaviour through building of human character. It is very easy to criticise others for their acts of corruption, but that would not be the answer to the problem. We can hope to root out corruption from the world only if we are able to root the nefarious thing out of our own hearts and minds.[2]

Power and corruption go hand in hand, particularly in the societies which give highest consideration to materialise and hold spiritual and ethical values and standards at low ebb. Absolute power corrupt absolutely. The existence of vigours anti-corruption laws and anti-corruption agencies supposed to help in reducing this menace from the society. But, the lacunas of such laws and lack of Morality amongst the custodian of such laws leads to failure in achieving the objectives of anti-corruption laws. I he handling of the anti-corruption work by the ministries concerned, or even the centralization of this work within the Home Ministry is not a healthy practice. The administration cannot be a judge of its own conduct. Besides, in the public mind a feeling persists that departmental proceedings against higher officers are not generally encouraged.[3] So, we need an effective and unbiased treatment of corrupt people by changing the existing procedures and processes. The difficulty of getting equal and just treatment of corrupt public servants irrespective of class, cadre and position prompted the demand for public inquiries. In this respect the Santhanem Committee's recommendations, if accepted by the government will perhaps be more effective to remove such type of misdeeds at least to a greater extent.

Public violence is the basis of any anti-corruption strategy-Tightening of law and setting no of new institutions for investigation alone are not at all sufficient to combat corruption under the present situation of ever expanding corruption techniques. The real remedy for checking this evil lies much deeper. It lies with the public, which should be prepared to put up a stiff fight against it. For every corrupt official, there are hundreds of members of the public wanting to make use of him and to feed him. It will be difficult to tackle this growing evil unless we mobilize the best elements in society to fight it. In some of foreign countries like United Kingdom and U.S.A., anti-corruption bodies have done excellent work in educating the people and in gathering and coordinating their will to resist it and focussing it by exposing corrupt practices mercilessly. The setting up of such organisation in India *is* a vital necessity.

Corruption in India has so far unchecked. It starts from the top echelons and reaches the lowest ebb in the society with the result that one cannot think of living honestly even if one aspires and yearns to do so. Here individual's corruption is limited only by the limited scope he finds for it and willy nilly we all find some scope.

These days everyone talks of corruption in public life, without realising that corruption in public life is but a reflection of corruption in private life[4]. It is highly contagious disease that spreads from one to the other, till a whole group, community or a nation as a whole becomes contaminated. The vicious cycle of corruption being started at the top, it can be stopped only when legal or moral or social pressure can be applied to the political and economic elite to win elections, run their political parties and earn their business profits by honest means. It depends upon the changing of the quality of public life. The prosecution alone cannot be effective in eradicating or significantly reducing the corruption from public life, the crisis of moral values and ethical codes appeared much earlier than the State's intervention to regulate the crime of corruption in the society. So it becomes very much difficult to eradicate this malady by the belated intervention of the State. The quality of public life depends upon its organisational set up in maintaining ordered norms of society.

In an ideal society, all members find their personal needs gratified by living up to the rules of the society and the members are motivated to follow the normative system of that society. The individual's wish to control transactions for personal benefit coincides with the cultural and social pressures exerted from group sources. But, the prevailing circumstances in India to-day polluted the public life with hiking dishonestly and corruption. The social, political and psychological conditions are so prominent in India that nothing worsts without one's indulging in corruption, in one way or the other, willingly or unwillingly. It becomes impossible for an honest man to live in peace in India. The practices which have become routine in everything from taking bribe in lieu of doing something to get admission to a College will force one to turn dishonest. Corruption essentially started when the power of money was first felt together with influence and authority of any kind. In fact we have reached a stage in corruption where the extent of each individual's corruption is limited only by the limited scope he has to be corrupt. Willingly or unwillingly each one of us finds some scope for it.

Since corruption in India starts from the top - the political leadership being its fountainhead it becomes impossible to root out this evil from the society without changing the behaviour of individuals in a society particularly of elite classes. The path of integrity for creating an environment which will sternly discourage any temptation for corruption must come from within the ministry and Department. To SUM up the measures for improving the quality of public life, it may be stated that, the evolution of a social climate in which no public servant or a person holding a public office, unless he is wholly devoid of moral sense, will be tempted to stray from the path of integrity and resort to corruption. Prosecution of corrupt public servants can contribute little to improve the quality of public life.

REFERENCES

1. John, E. Monteiro (1966), *Corruption*, p. 111.
2. Mital Memisharan (1991), *World Famous Corrupt Politicians*, p. 26.
3. Monteiro, John. B. (1966), *Corruption*, p. 109.
4. Kohli, S. (1975), *Corruption—The Growing Evil in India*, p. 26.

6

Judicial Findings

Trial of corruption cases in the Courts provides some valuable informations on the gravity and extent of this white collar crime existed in the society.

Supreme Court Cases

State of Madras -V- A. Vaidyanatha Iyer A.I.R., 1958; S.C. 61

The charge against the respondent, an Income Tax Officer was that he had obtained from the complainant Rs. 800.00 as gratification other than legal remuneration as a motive for the reward for showing favour to him in the exercise of the official functions. The explanation of the respondent was that he mentioned to the complainant about his money difficulties when accidentally he meet him, on the road. The complainant offered to lend him Rs. 1000.00 for which a pronote was to be executed by the respondent. The complainant paid Rs. 800.00 in the morning, and promised to pay Rs. 200.00 in the evening. The respondent had the pronote ready and offered to hand it over in the morning, but the complainant paid he would take it when he left the house.

The raiding party had recovered the amount of Rs. 800/ from the accused which he had produced from the folds of his 'dhoti'. The special Judge accepted the story of prosecution and found the accused respondent guilty. The High Court acquitted the respondent and mentioned in the judgement " in any case, the evidence is not enough to show that the explanation offered by the accused cannot reasonably be true, and so the benefit of doubt must go to him." Kapur, J. speaking for the Supreme Court observed that the above passage from judgement is indicative of a disregard of the presumption which the law requires to be raised under Sec. 4. It is a presumption of law and therefore it is obligatory on the court to raise this presumption in every case brought under Sec. 4 of the Prevention of Corruption Act, because unlike the case of presumption of fact, presumption law constitutes a breach of jurisprudence, while giving the finding quoted above, the learned judge seems to have disregarded the special rule of burden of proof under Sec. 4 and therefore his approach in this case has been on erroneous lines.

C.I. Emden -V- State of U.P. A.I.R. 1960; S.C. 548; 2 S.C.R. 592,1960

The appellant was a Loco foreman at Loco Shed and had secured a contract at the same place for the removal of cinders from ash pits and for loading coal. The R demanded from S Rs. 400/ per month in order that S may be allowed to carry out his, contract peacefully without any harassment. S was told by the appellant that he had been receiving a monthly payment from R who had held a similar contract before his and that it would be to his interest to agree to pay the bribe. S however refused to accede to this request and that led to many hostile acts on the part of the appellant. After some time, the appellant again asked S to pay him the monthly bribe as already suggested. S then requested him to reduce the demand on the ground that the contract given to him was for a much lesser amount than that which had given to his predecessor R; the appellant thereupon agreed to accept Rs. 375/. S had no money at that time and so he asked for time to make the necessary arrangement. The agreement then was that S would pay the money to the appellant on January 8. Meanwhile S approached the Deputy superintendent of Police, Corruption Branch. S s statement was then recorded by a Magistrate and it was decided to lay a trap. The trap was laid S gave the money to appellant on his demand and raiding party on getting information immediately arrived on the spot. Then Magistrate disclosed his identity to the appellant and asked him to produce the amount paid to him by S The appellant then took out the currency notes from his pocket and handed them over to the Magistrate. It is on these facts that charges under Sec. 161 of I.P.C. and Sec, 5 (2) of the Prevention of Corruption Act, were framed against the appellant. The appellant denied the charges, he admitted that he had received Rs. 375/ from S but his case was that, at his request S had advanced the said amount to him by way of loan. Gajendragadkar J. held that the High Court was justified in raising the presumption against the appellant, because it is admitted by him that he received Rs. 375/ from S and that the amount thus received by him was other than legal remuneration.

V.D. Jhingam -V- State of U.P. A.I.R. 1966; S.C. 1762, 1966

At the time of recovery of the money the appellant made a statement that, amount received by him was a loan as he wanted to purchase a bunglow. His defence was that he never negotiated regarding the bribe and had been falsely implicated in order to take revenge. The question for determination was whether a presumption under sub-section (1) of Sec. 4 of the Prevention of Corruption Act, arises in this case. Held, the plain meaning of this clause undoubtedly requires the presumption to be raised whenever it is shown that the valuable thing has been received by the accused without anything more. If that is the position in respect of the construction of this part of Sec. 4 (l) it would be unreasonable to hold that the word 'gratification' in the same clause imports the necessity to prove not only the payment of money, but the incriminating character of the said payment.

State of Assam -V- Krishna Rao and Another. A.I.R. 1973; S.C. 28

It was held by Dua J. speaking for the Supreme Court that when the evidence of the recovery of money from the pockets of the pants of the accused persons has been accepted and upheld by both the courts, then by virtue of Sec. 4 of The prevention of Corruption Act, the courts were legally obliged to raise the presumption that the two accused persons had accepted or obtained or agreed to accept or attempted to obtain that money as a motive or reward such as is mentioned in Sec. 161 I.P.C. unless the contrary was proved. If money were recovered from, the pockets of the accused persons which were not their legal remuneration then the material on the record, there can be no further question of showing that these monies had been consciously received by them, because the defence version that these money had been thrust into their pockets is on the face of it, wholly unsatisfactory, unreasonable if not filmsy.

State of Rajasthan -V- Mohammed Habib A.I.R. 1973; CR.L.J 703

Where a public servant obtains from the complainant the amount recovered from him during the trap and he fails to offer explanation, the following conclusions of Lodha J. is that he had accepted the amount as gratification as envisaged under Sec, 151, I.P.C. and under Sec. 4 (l) of The Prevention of Corruption Act.

Bhupesh Deb Gupta -V- state of Tripura A.I.R. 1978; S.C. 1672,1978; Cr.L.J. 1738, 1978

The chargesheet against the appellant stated that the amount was remitted for showing favour in exercise of his official function, but what was sought to be made out was that the gratification was paid to the accused for influencing a public servant, held the presumption under Sec. 4 (1) cannot arise.

Banshilal- V - State of Bihar A.I.R. 1981; S.C. 1235, 1981; Cr.L.J. 741, 1981

Where the accused when examined under Sec 315 Cr.P.C. stated that Currency notes were trusted in his pocket, that statement by itself without anything more is not sufficient to satisfy the necessary ingredients of Sec. 4 (1) that accused accepted or attempted to obtain or has agreed to accept or attempt to obtain, any gratification other than legal remuneration so as to be able to raise the presumption.

Pandurang Laxman -V- State of Bombay A.I.R. 1959, Bombay 30

The accused appellant was a watchman in the employ of Bombay Port Trust. The complainant one G was a driver of a bullock cart which belongs to his master, one M. He used to stay in an area which belongs to the Bombay Port Trust. G used to drive the bullock cart on hire. The accused asked G not to keep the bullock cart there or to give him an amount of Rs. 10/ per month as bribe. G agreed to pay an amount of Rs. 10/ per month and he made two such payments. When he could not pay he approached the Anti-Corruption Branch and his complaint was recorded. A trap was laid and the amount of Rs. 8/ -paid by G was recovered from the accused. The accused admitted that he had received the amount, but he did not receive it as a bribe or illegal gratification, but it was loan returned by G. Held, that the complainant himself is a partisan witness in such cases and it is well settled that it is not safe to rely upon the uncorroborated testimony of such a witness. A mere payment without more would not amount to a gratification other than legal remuneration and if it does not amount to a gratification other than legal remuneration, there is no scope for raising presumption under Sec. 4 of the P.C. Act.

Kunhi-V -State A.I.R. 1959, Kerela 88

The accused was one of the assistant goods clerks of Trichur Goods shed. P.W.2 who used to send goods by railway from Trichur, sent a petition to the railway authorities complaining that corruption was rampant among the clerks of Trichur Goods Shed end making specific allegations against one G who was a Booking clerk and the accused and that if the railway authorities took no action, the petitioner would be forced to take action himself against the erring clerks. P.W.2 had to send 57 bags, of these he sent 30 bags on 14th and the remaining 27 bags were to be sent on 23 rd. At the time of booking of 30 bags, the accused and G demanded a mamool or illegal gratification at the rate of 2 annas per bag. As P.W.2 had then no sufficient money with him he said that he would pay the mamool for the entire 57 bags on, 23 rd when the remaining begs were to be booked. P.W. 2 went to P.W. 1, the investigation officer of the Delhi special police Establishment who at that time was stationed at Trichur and gave him a written complaint. P.W.12 obtained the sanction of Special First Class Magistrate to investigate the case under the prevention of Corruption Act, and held a trap for the accused. On completion of documents for the booking of 27 bags, the accused demanded the mamool and when he stretched his hand, P.W. 2 pieced the money in the hand of the accused. On receiving money, the accused went out for about two minutes during which time he bought a lottery ticket for Rs. 2/ and he was just returning to the shed by one door that by another door P.W. 12 also entered the shed and asked P.W.2 who was K, and P.W.2 pointed out the accused, Seeing this the accused hastly went out of the shed and P.W. 12 followed him celling out his name and caught him as he was running round a cart which was on the platform. While he was thus running the accused took some currency notes from his pocket and threw them away and after he was caught, P.W. 12's orderly picked them up from the platform on P.W. 12's order. Four one rupee currency notes thus picked up and one rupee note recovered from the pocket where the notes produced by P.W. 2 earlier in the day for which a mahassar had been prepared before making the raid. The accused pleaded not guilty and stated in Court that P.W. 2 gave the money to him to give it to G. The Session Judge disbelieved this plea and convicted the accused under Sec. 161 I.P.C. and 5 (l) (d) read with Sec. 5 (2) of the P.C. Act.

G. Kumara Pillai J. held that a presumption under Sec. 4 (1) of The Prevention of Corruption Act, arises on these facts against the accused. The burden is on the accused to disprove the presumption, The degree of proof required to rebut the presumption must of course, depend upon the facts and circumstances of each case. As the contrary has to be proved, it will not be sufficient for the accused merely to create a doubt.

Dhanavantrai Bahwantrai -V- State of Maharastra A.I.R. 1964 S.C. 575

It was a case where the appellant before the High Court, a Resident Engineer for Light Houses was charged and convicted under Sec. 161 I.P.C., and Sec. 5 (1) (d) of The Prevention of Corruption Act, read with Sec. 5 (2) thereof. He was alleged to have accepted Rs. 1000/ as illegal gratification. The receipt of the amount was admitted by the appellant. The defence was that he had accepted the said amount, to be handed over to the temple authorities for carrying out certain repairs which the complainant had undertaken to do and which he was not able to carry out and had instead given the amount to the appellant with a request that the amount be given over to the temple authorities as compensation. The defence was not accepted by the trial court as well as the High Court. It was contended before the Supreme Court on behalf of the appellant, that an accused person is entitled to rebut even the presumption arising by virtue of a statutory provision, by merely offering an explanation which is reasonable and probable. The Supreme Court rejected the contention The court pointed out that the burden resting on an accused person in a case where Sec. 4 of The Prevention of Corruption Act applied would not be as light as it is where a presumption is raised under Sec. 114 of the Evidence Act, and cannot be held to be discharged merely by reason of the fact that the explanation offered by the accused is reasonable and probable. It must further be shown that the explanation is true one. The words 'unless the contrary is proved' which occur in this provision make it clear that the presumption has to be rebutted by proof and not by a bare explanation which is merely plausible. A fact is said to be proved where its existence is directly established or when upon the material before it, the court finds its existence to be so probable that a reasonable man would set on the supposition that it exists. Unless therefore the explanation is supported by proof, the presumption created by the provision cannot be said to be rebutted. It further held that the question whether a presumption of law or facts stands rebutted by evidence or other material on record is one of fact and not of law.

Deonath Dudbnath Mishra -V- State of Maharastra, A.I.R. 1957: Bombay 1

The appellant was the reader to the sub-divisional officer. The complainant (P.W 1) who has been holding a license for possession and sale of explosives, has applied to the sub-Divisional Officer for a renewal of the license after adding more villages therein. The S.D.O. was authorised by the District Magistrate to renew such licenses, but without lacking any alteration therein, Since an alteration was prayed for by way of inserting some other villages, the license was forwarded to the district Magistrate. The license however was not received back from the District legislate for several months find P.W.1 during this period went five or six times to the office of the S.D.O. to get the license, if received back. This time when P.W.1 approached the appellant and enquired from him about the license, the appellant told P.W. 1 that he would give the same immediately if Rs. 5/ by way of illegal gratification were paid to him, P.W. 1 ostensibly agreed to pay the amount, but did not like the idea and therefore, approached the Anti-Corruption Police and gave his complaint. The Magistrate granted permission for investigation of offence. Thereafter a trap was laid, as usual, the currency notes were dusted with anthrances powder and handed over to P.W. 1. P.W.1 went to the appellant who replied that he had not seen the dak received that day, he would take action on receipt of license. The appellant asked P.W.1 to give him Rs. 5/ for sending the license by post to his address after it was received. In accordance with that demand, P.W.1 paid the marked notes of Rs. 5/ to the appellant in the presence of the panch. Upon the agreed signal being given, P.S. 1 came there and called the appellant out. He examined the hands of the appellant under the ultra-violet lamp and on finding that there were trace of anthrance powder, called upon the appellant to produce the amount which he had received from P.W. 1. The appellant handed over to the P.S. 1 the marked currency notes. The S.D.O. who had been called out also saw the appellant giving those notes to the P.S.I. The appellant was prosecuted under Sec. 161 I.P.C. and Sec. 5 (1) (d) read with Sec. 5 (2) of the P.C. Act and was convicted by the special Judge under both the counts. Held, the Special Judge has considered at great length, the evidence in order to determine whether a demand for such an illegal gratification and the payment thereof were or were not probable. All that unnecessary discussion could have been easily avoided if the legal presumption under Sec. 4 (1) of the P.C. Act Lad been raised on finding that the prosecution had established that the amount of Rs. 5/ was paid to the appellant otherwise than as legal remuneration. Held further that it would not be permissible or possible to accept the defence on the basis that it say be reasonable or proper. It is not sufficient for the accused to merely put forth a reasonable or probable story, but that the explanation of the accused must be supported by proof within the meaning of Sec. 3 of the Indian Evidence Act. Nothing of the sort has been done in the present case, consequently, it must be held that the presumption was not rebutted.

C.N. Peters -V- The State, A.I.R. 1959, Allahabad 483

The appellant was posted at Gorakhpur as the Claim prevention Inspector, K was a guard in the same railway. K had taken a goods train from Gonde to Gorakhpur and when the train reached Gorakhpur, it was found that some bags were stolen away from one of the wagons in the train. A report was made to Government Railway Police and enquired the matter accordingly. The appellant joined this enquiry on his own. The appellant demanded Rs. 300/ from K as illegal gratification telling him that he will give a favourable report, but this money was not paid to him, he will give an adverse report. K gave a written report to Special Police Establishment and a trap was laid. The moment the money was handed over and pocketted by the appellant, the Inspector of Police took the search of appellant and Rs. 300/ were recovered from the pocket of appellant. The appellant admitted the recovery of Rs. 330/ from his pocket, but has been changing his defence. A.N. Mulla J. held that once the prosecution established the receipt of the tainted money by an accused person, then the onus is cast on the accused to rebut the presumption against him and offer an explanation. A presumption therefore, arose against the appellant and it was for him to rebut this presumption which he has failed to do by taking several stands.

Ram Dulare Yadav -V- State of U.P., Cr.L.J. 988 (Allahabad), 1971

No case of criminal nature had been registered at the Police outpost where the appellant was posted as a constable nor had the appellant been deputed by the Head Constable of Police outpost to make any enquiry into the affairs of the alleged theft. The appellant brought one S to the police outpost on a false charge of receiving stolen property and after threats managed to get from him Rs 27/. Held the offence was not covered by Sec. 5 of P.C. Act, but was extortion.

Dalpat Singh -V- State of Rajasthan, A.I.R. 1969; S.C. 17, 1969; Cr.L.J. 262 (1968)

The appellant conspired to extort money as well as other valuable things from the villagers by using force or threat of force or by harassment. Neither the appellants intended to show any official favour to the person from whom they extorted money or valuable things nor these persons expected any official favour from them They paid the amounts in question solely with a view to avoid being ill treated or harassed. Therefore it is difficult to hold that the acts complained against the appellants can be held constitute offences under Sec. 161 I.P.C.

Jaswant Singh -V- State of Punjab, A.I.R. 1973; S.C. 707, 1973

The appellant was convicted by the High Court on the evidence of the complainant corroborated by the evidence of the police officers. The evidence of the Police Officers showed that - (i) when the police party stopped the rickshaw, the appellant threw the currency notes which fell on the footboard of the rickshaw, (ii) the currency notes were seized and (iii) the numbers of the seized currency notes tallied with the records already made.

It was held by the Supreme Court that ——

1. The evidence of the complainant will have to be considered with great caution and it will not be ordinarily safe to accept his interested testimony unless there is material corroboration found in the other evidence adduced by the prosecution.
2. Such evidence is available in this case.
3. Though there is some discrepancy in the evidence of the police officers regarding -
   (a) the actual number of notes that were still in the hand of the accused and
   (b) the number that had fallen on the footboard of the rickshaw and
   (c) which officer caught hold of which arm of the accused

Those are all very minor discrepancies which do not effect their evidence regarding

(i) the throwing of the notes by the appellant and
(ii) their seizure by the police officers.

Moba Singh -V- State (Delhi Administration; A.I.R 1976; S.C. 449, 1976; Cr.L.J. 346 (1976)

The accused appellant, a head Constable in Police stood charged under Sec. 7 (old Sec. 161 I.P.C.) and Sec. 13 (2) (old Sec. 5 (2)) read with Sec. 13 (1) (d) (old Sec. 5 (1) (d)8) of the Prevention of Corruption Act. According to the prosecution, the accused had earlier negotiated for a bribe and later on, accepted the same from the complainant. According to the accused, he made no negotiation with the complainant nor did he voluntarily accept any money from the complainant. On the other hand the complainant planted the currency note of Rs. 10/ into his pocket against his wishes when he was all of a sudden surrounded by the Anti-corruption Inspector and the raiding party. It was held by the Supreme Court that-

1. If the accused's version is true the recovery of the note would have been inside 'purchee' since the accused and his four supporter witnesses had deposed to that effect. If this version is even prima facie reliable, the accused will be entitled to the benefit of doubt. However it cannot be held so.

The seizure memo shows that a currency note of Rs. 10/ was recovered from the left side front pocket of the shirt worn by the accused. There is nothing to show that this currency note was recovered from his pocket being wrapped inside the particular 'purchee'. The defence story of the complainant giving a ten rupee note wrapped inside the purchee' is absolutely false.

The evidence of the complainant is corroborated by the inspector and P.W.3 and also by the documentary evidence, coupled with the manner of the recovery of the none. When there is such a conclusive proof with regard to this part of the case, deficiency of evidence of corroboration with regard to the negotiation of the accused with the complainant falls into insignificance.

2. When witnesses swear home through a two inch board and sometimes quantitatively the defence masters up a number of witnesses, the court has to be extremely cautions and careful to enter a verdict of guilty only if the complainant's version is supported by some clinching circumstances of such character and quality as may reasonably assure the judicial mind about the truth of the real position against the accused. 3. The defence plea of planting of any incriminating object in answer to a charge, to be successful, must be, or at any rato, should reasonably appear to have been made without the knowledge or acquiescence of the accused. The case in hand is not such a case.

R.G. Jacob -V- Republic of India, A.I.R. 1963; S.C. 550.1963 (3) S.C.R. 800 (1963)

One N a merchant having export business in chillies made on application for export of chillies, He was informed by a letter that hie application had been rejected. The letter was signed by the assistant Controller of Exports for the Joint Chief Controller of Imports and Exports. A who had been acting on behalf of N in this matter met the appellant who was the Assistant Controller of Imports in the office of the Joint Chief Controller of Imports and Exports. The appellant told A that an appeal would have to be preferred against the rejection order to the Joint Chief Controller of Imports and Exports. The appellant also proposed that if he was given two bags of cement and Rs. 50/ he would use his influence and help him to get him the permit. A agreed and the appellant gave A a sheet of paper stating the address to which the cement was to be sent. On the next date memorandum of appeal was sent by registered post to the Joint Chief controller of Imports and Exports. The same day A saw the Deputy Superintendent, Special Police Establishment, and gave him a complaint in writing mentioning the facts. A trap was thereafter laid with a view to catch the appellant in the actual act of accepting the bribe. The bags of cement and Rs. 80/ were recovered from the house of appellant. The appellant was tried by the Special Judge on charges under. Sec. 161 I.P.C. Sec 5 (1) (d) read with See. 5 (2) of P.C. Act and Sec. 65, I.P.C. He was acquitted of the first two charges, but convicted of an offence under Sec. 165 I..P.C. The high Court dismissed the appeal of appellant. All the other ingredients of an offence under Sec. 165 I.P.C. had been proved prima facie and the appeal was mainly on the point whether appellant was subordinate to the Joint Chief Controller of Imports and Exports. Held, the word' has been used by the Legislature without any limitation. by the use of the word 'subordinate' without any qualifying words, the Legislature has expressed its legislative intention of making punishable such subordinates also who have no connection with the functions with which the business or transaction is concerned, The appellant has rightly been held to be subordinate' to the Joint Chief Controller of Imports and Exports even though the appellant had no function to discharge in connection with the appeal before Joint Chief Controller of Imports and Exports.

R.S. Nayak -V - A.R. Antulay, A.I.R. 1980 S.C. 2045,1986, Cr.L.J. 1922

The appellant filed a complaint in the court of Chief Metropolitan Magistrate against the respondent, who was then Chief Minister of Maharashtra, alleging that the accused in his capacity as Chief Minister and thereby a public servant within the meaning of Sec. 21, I.P.C. had committed offences under Sec. 161, 165, I.P.C. and Sec. 5 of the 1947 Act, Sec. 384 and Sec. 420, I.P.C. read with Sec. 109 and 120-B, I.P.C. The Magistrate held that the complaint relating to the alleged offences under Sec. 161 and 165 I.P.C. and Sec. 6 of the Act was not maintainable in absence of the requisite sanction under Sec 6 of the Act. The respondent submitted his resignation from his office of the Chief Minister on January 12, 1982 and he ceased to hold that office with effect from January 20, 1982, but continued to be sitting MLA. On April 12, 1982, a special criminal appeal filed by the complainant appellant against the order of the Magistrate was dismissed by the High Court. An appeal by special leave filed by the State under Article 136 against the High Court's decision was rejected by the Supreme Court on July 28, 1982 by its decision in the State of Maharashtra -V- R.S. Kayak (1982) 2 SCC; 463 1382 SCC (Cri)478. Thereupon the Governor of Maharashtra on the same day granted the sanction under Sec. 6 of the Act, to prosecute the accused in respect of specific charges set out in the order according sanction. The complainant then filed a fresh complaint on Aug. 9, 1982 against the accused respondent in the Court of Special Judge, Bombay. The Special Judge took cognizance of offence on the same day and issued process. The case was later transferred to another special Judge who ultimately by his order dated July 25, 1983 uphold the contention of the accused that even though the accused had ceased to be the Chief minister, on the date of taking cognizance of the offence, he was a sitting member of the Maharashtra Legislative Assembly and as such a public servant within the meaning of Sec. 21 I.P.C. and that unless a sanction to prosecute him by the authority competent to remove him from his office as MLA was obtained which in the opinion of the Special Judge was the Maharashtra Legislative Assembly the accused was entitled to be discharged. The Supreme Court allowed the appeal, set aside the order and decision of the Special Judge and directed that the trial should proceed further from the stage where the accused was discharged. Held,

As the contentions canvassed before this Court are mainly questions of law, facts at this stage having a peripheral relevance in the course of discussion, it is unnecessary to set out the prosecution case as disclosed in the complaint filed by complainant Ramdas Shrinivas Nayak (complainant for short) in detail save and except, few pertinent and relevant allegations.

It was contended that the question whether a person "in the pay of the 'Government " is ipso facto a public servant in no *more* res integra and concluded by the decision of the Constitution bench in Kerunanidni case, (M. Karunanidhi - V- Union of India, 1979; 3 SCR 254, 3SCC 431, 1979; SCC 'Cri' 691; 1979 Cr.L.J. 773). The court further observed that the expression in the pay of connotes that a person in getting salary, compensation, wages or any amount of money This by itself however, does not lead to the inference that a relationship of master and servant must necessarily exist in all cases where a person is paid salary the phrase " In the pay of the government " does not import of necessity a master-servant relationship. It is perfectly possible to say that a person can be in the pay of the government if he is paid in consideration of discharging an assignment entrusted to *him* by the government without there necessarily being a master-servant relationship between them. It is not unused in common parlance to speak of a person being in the pay of another if he is paid for acting at the behest or according to the desire of the other without the other being his master and he the servant, that is to say without the control over the manner of doing the work which a master-servant relationship implies. It is such a category in addition to the one "in the service of the government" that is sought to be comprehended in clause (12) (a) In respect of the extracted observation of the Constitution Bench, there is no attempt to distinguish the decision in karunanidhi case and therefore, it is not necessary to consider the decisions cited in support of the submission that a Judgement of the Supreme Court especially of the Constitution Bench cannot be distinguished lightly and is binding on us and unless questions of fundamental importance to national life are involved, need not be re-examined.

It was also contended that MLA is not performing any public duty. It is not necessary to examine this aspect because it would be rather difficult to accept an unduly wide submission that M LA is not performing any public duty. However it is unquestionable that he is not performing any public duty either directed by the government or for the government. He no doubt performs public duties cast on him by the Constitution and his electorate. He thus discharges Constitutional functions for which he is remunerated by fees under the Constitution and not *by* the Executive.

If MLA is not in the pay of the Government in the sense of Executive Government or is not remunerated by fees for performance of any public duly by the Executive Government, certainly he would not be comprehended in the expression 'public servant' within the meaning *at* the expression in clause (12) (a), He is thus not a public servant within the meaning of the expression in clause (12) (a).

To sum up the learned Special Judge was clearly in error in holding that MLA is a public servant within the meaning of expression in section 12 (a) and further, error in holding that sanction of the Legislative Assembly of Maharastra or majority of the members was a condition precedent to taking cognizance of offences committed by the accused, for the reasons herein stated both the conclusions are wholly unsustainable and must be quashed and set aside. This appeal accordingly succeeds and is allowed. The order and decision of the learned Special Judge Sri R.B. Sule dated July 25,1963 discharging the accused in Special case No. 24 of 1982 and Special case No. 3/83 is thereby set aside and the trial shall proceed further from the stage where the accused was discharged.

The accused was the Chief Minister of a premier State - the State of Maharastra. By a prosecution launched as early as on Sept, 11, 1981, his character and integrity come under a cloud. Nearly 24 years have rolled by and the case has not moved in inch further. An expeditious trial is primarily in the interest of the accused and a mandate of article 21. expeditious disposal of a criminal case is in the interest of both, the prosecution and the accused. Therefore, Special case No. 24 of 1982 and Special case No.3 of 1983 pending in the court of Special Judge, Greater Bombay, Sri R.B. Sule are withdrawn and transferred to the High Court of Bombay with a request to the learned Chief Justice to assign these two cases to a sitting judge of the High Court. On being so assigned, the learned judge may proceed to expeditious dispose of the cases preferably by holding the trial from day to day.

Order in Transferred Case 356 of 1983

Petitioner Abdul Rehman Antulay preferred Criminal Revision Application No. 363 of 1983 against that pert of the order of Special Judge, by which his contention that there was error in taking cognisance of the offences when accused No.2 is, described as persons Known and unknown. This Criminal Revision application stands transferred in this Court. It was heard alongwith this group of matters, there is no substance in any of the contentions raised in the criminal revision application and the same is rejected.

Order in Writ Petition (Criminal) No. 1145 of 1983

This writ petition was filed by the original complainant Cri R.S. Nayak questioning the decision of the Special judge that a private complainant is not maintainable. In view of the decision in criminal appeal No. 356 of 1983 with transferred case No. 347 of 1983 and 348 of 1983, this petition does not survive and stands disposed of as infractuous.

Order in Civil Writ Petition No. 4227 of 1983

This writ petition was filed by Sri A.R. Antulay challenging the Constitutional validity of section 6 of the P.C. Act, 1947. Mr. Singhvi learned counsel who appeared for the petitioner sought permission to withdraw the petition and accordingly the petition is disposed of as withdrawn.

Bal Krishna Sayal -V- State of Punjab, A.I.R. 1987, S.C. 669 (From Punjab)

Where in a case of bribe it was alleged that for waiver of penal rent which was found to be Rs. 102/ in respect of official residence of the complainant he offered a bribe of Rs. 100/ it was held that to obtain waiver of the rent it was unlikely that a bribe of Rs. 100/ would have been offered. Thus it could not be said that the offence was proved beyond reasonable doubt. Also there was no clear evidence about what talk preceded the passing of the currency notes. It cannot be said that even if the prosecution had not indicated what exactly the conversation was once the passing of the currency notes was accepted, it was for the accused to exclaim the circumstances under which the same had been received. Criminal appeal So. 1031 of 1973 Dt. 11.4.77 revised.

Ranganath Misra, J. - This appeal is by special leave and the affirming judgement of the Punjab and Haryana High Court upholding the convictions and sentences of the appellant under S.5 (2) of the P.C. Act and S. 161 of the I.P.C. is sought to be set aside.

The appellant was a clerk in the Prescribed Branch of the Divisional superintendent, Northern Railway at Firozpur, one Gurucharan Ram, a fitter in the railway establishment had become liable to penal rent in respect of the official residence occupied by him. The prosecution alleged that the appellant demanded a bribe of Rs. 100/ from Gurucharan Ram to obtain an order of waiver of the penal rent. G. Ram pleaded that he was not in a position to pay the amount demanded and it was ultimately settled that the sum of Rs. 100/ would be paid in five instalments of Rs. 20/ each. With reference to the payment of the first instalment of Rs. 20/, a trap was laid and soon after the bribe had been received, the trap party recovered the amount. The defence was one of total denial.

Two outsider witnesses had been examined in the case being Khazen Singh and Ram Chander in support of the case. Khazen Singh as notified by the High Court did not speak us to what transpired in the conversation between the bribe giver and the appellant. The other witness was also not very clear as to what talk preceded the passing of the two currency notes.

The High Court took the view that even if the prosecution had not indicated what exactly the conversation was once the passing two currency notes was accepted, it was for the appellant to explain the circumstances under which the same had been received. Another contention which had been raised before the High Court was that the total penal rent due from G. Ram was Rs. 102/ and to obtain waiver of this it was unlikely that R. Ram would have agreed to pay a sum of Rs. 100/ as above. He wanted to find out exactly how much of penal rent was due and therefore sent for the record. From the record it is apparent that the demand was Rs. 102/ which G. Ram wanted to be waived. There is, no material to show whether there was likelihood of any additional demand to be raised against him. Taking the unsatisfactory character of the prosecution evidence in regard to the conversation proceeding, the passing of the currency notes and the feature that for waiver of Rs. 102/ the bribe of Rs. 100/ was offered, we are inclined to take the view that the prosecution has failed to establish its case beyond reasonable doubt and the appellant is entitled to this benefit of this situation. The appeal is allowed and the conviction and the sentences are set aside.

State of U.P. -V- Dr. G.R. Ghosh, A.I.R. 1984; S.C. 1452: 1983 All. L.J. 1170

Where an accused person - a government Doctor- was convicted by the Session Court for accepting illegal gratification and the high Court acquitted aim on the ground the official might have demanded and accepted the amount as by way of his professional fees inasmuch as a government Doctor was permitted to have private practice of his own as per the relevant rules, though such was not his defence at any stage.

Held that the High Court reported to surmises and conjectures for which there was not the slightest basis, apart from the fact that no such defence was taken and no such plea was ever advanced by the accused. Under the circumstances the decision of the High Court cannot be sustained or; the basis of the reasoning which found favour with it.

The prosecution case is as under-Respondent was an orthopaedic Surgeon in the UHM Hospital at Kanpur. He was in charge of the orthopaedic department, in his capacity as a Government Medical Officer he was allowed an official residence within the campus of the hospital. As per the then prevailing rules, he was permitted consolation practice at his residence in the evening. One Kumari Ramsri, 13. year old daughter of P.W. 3, Babu Lal, a worker employed in a parachute factory as a packer was suffering from Bone T.B. and was admitted to the UMH Hospital on 18th Feb. 1976. She was referred to the Orthopaedic section on 19th Feb. 1976. She was pieced under the treatment of respondent Dr. Ghosh. After about six or seven days the respondent asked P.W.3 to remove the patient from the Hospital saying that she was cured. P.W.3 objected saying that the condition of his child had not improved. The respondent asked. P.W.3 to see him at his residence in the evening. It appears that at the Hospital Babu Lal learnt that he would have to pay some money to the respondent Dr. Ghosh, if he wanted his child to be treated properly. P.W. 3 therefore paid Rs. 20/ to the respondent when he called on him at his residence in the evening as suggested earlier. Thereupon the respondent told P.W.3 that his child would be permitted to remain in the hospital for treatment. Even so some seven or eight days later the respondent asked P.W.3 to remove the child from the hospital. It appears that P.W.3 gathered the impression that he would have to pay money to the respondent for obtaining proper treatment at the hospital. P.W.3 in this background made a request to the respondent to issue a certificate so that he could get a loan or advance for the medical expenses. The respondent told P.W.3 that he would have to pay a sum of Rs. 250/ to obtain a certificate to enable him to obtain a loan of Rs. 500/. P.W.3 refused to accede to the demand. Thereupon the respondent told him to remove the patient from the hospital. In view of what transpired, P.W.3 met the respondent on March 13, 1976, and requested him to issue a certificate to enable him to obtain a loan from the factory. The respondent again told him that he would not issue a certificate unless his demand for Rs. 250/ was met. P.W.3 made entreaties to the respondent, but the respondent did not relent. He told him to remove the patient from the hospital. Thereupon P.W. 3 promised to the respondent that he would make some payment immediately and that the remaining amount would be paid shortly thereafter. P.W.3 went back to bring the money. It appears that he felt exasperated and conceived the idea of trapping the respondent at this juncture. He had five currency notes of the denomination of its. 10/ with him. He noted down the numbers of these notes and carried the sum with him when he again approached the respondent. The respondent accepted the five currency notes, but refused to issue a certificate unless the remaining amount of Rs. 200/ was paid to him, though P.W. promised to pay the remaining amount within three or four days. P.W.3 was thereupon very much annoyed by the attitude of the respondent and he decided to approach the vigilance Dept. He approached the vigilance officer and lodged complaint exhibit KA-8 on March 31,1976. It appears that he has borrowed Rs. 200/ with a view to provide the currency notes for laying trap. He had carried 20 ten rupee notes with him. In the complaint lodged by him, Exhibit KA-8, he specified the number of the five ten rupee notes which he had already given to the respondent on the earlier occasion the numbers of which he had noted down previously. He also specified the numbers of the 20 ten rupee notes provided by him at the time of lodging the complaint. The Superintendent of vigilance Dept., Sri I.P. Bhatnagar called his deputy, Dy. J.P. Pandey and asked him to do the needful in the matter. Dy. S.P. Pandey asked P.W.3 to meet him on Aug. 2, 1976 at 5.30 P.M. in Kaushik Park meanwhile Superintendent Bhatnagar contacted the Director of vigilance Dept. and moved the complaint to the competent authority for the requisite permission. The Commissioner-cum Secretary of the vigilence Dept. Sri Khodati granted written permission to lay a trap against the respondent. On receiving the sanction, Superintendent Bhatnagar directed dy. S.P Pandey to proceed to lay the trap. It is the prosecution case that thereafter P.W.3 contacted Dy. S.P. pandey at kaushik Park on April 2, 1976 at 5.30 P.M Two witnesses were called. The currency notes were handed over to P.W.1, Inspector Bahadur Singh. Initials were made on the 20 G.C. notes, the notes were treated with Phenolphthalin powder and the plan of the trap was explained to P.W.3, the public witnesses, and to the members who were to accompany the party.

As per the plan, initially, Sham Lal and Thakur prasad were sent to the consultation room of the respondent on the second floor of his residence. What transpired need not be stated as he has not been examined as a witness. After sham Lal returned, P.W.3 along with P.W.2 constable Bachu Lal entered the consultation room. P.W.2 was in plain clothes and had posed as the elder brother of P.W.3. When both of them entered the consultation room, respondent enquired from P.. 3 whether he had brought the money. P.W.3 replied in the affirmative. P.W.3 then handed over the 20 ten rupee notes which had been treated with the powder and the numbers of which had been noted down in the complaint against the respondent. The respondent took these notes in his hands and placed the same in the left front pocket of the bush shirt. Thereafter, took the form on which he was to issue the certificate from P.W.3 and started filling in the details. The form was a typed one and there were blank spares which were required to be filed in.

The High Court set aside the finding under a serious misconception on an altogether untenable reasoning which even the counsel for the respondent has not been able to support, turning to the question of sentence having regard to the fact that the respondent had to undergo the tension of a pending trial and a pending appeal for six years, and the fact that it will have adverse impact on his employment after 23 years of service, no useful purpose would be served by imposing a long term of jail sentence. The substantive sentence of two years R.I. is therefore reduced to one of 5 months R.I. The appeal is accordingly allowed, the order of acquittal rendered by the High Court is set aside, and the finding of guilt and the order of conviction recorded by the learned Special Judge is resorted, but the sentence is modified to the aforesaid extent. The respondent shall surrender to bail in order to undergo the substantive sentence imposed on him. Appeal allowed.

Brij Lal Srivastava -V- State of M.P., A.I.R. 1379; S.C. 1080, (1979) 4SCC 521; 1979 Cr.L.J. 913

The appellant was the Principal of a Higher Secondary School. The main charge against him was that:

1. On 6.3.1964 he had drawn certain sum on the contingent bill for various items.
2. One of the items was the salary of chowkidar (P.W.9) for ten months at the rate of Rs. 50/ p.m. the total amount being Rs. 500/.
3. The Chowkidar was never employed in the School and the appellant had merely drawn this amount to misappropriate it.
4. A receipt (Ex P-26) was given by P who has admitted his signature on this receipt. Nowhere in his evidence he said that he did not receive the money from the appellant or that the receipt was forcibly taken by

the appellant without paying him any money. He admitted that he used to work at the House of the appellant.

5. The Special judge convicted the appellant and the High Court confirmed the conviction was held by the Supreme Court that -

   (a) Admittedly the gardener and Rambai worked in the school, but their names were also not found in the attendance Register. The amount withdrawn by the appellant in respect of the expenses incurred for them was not doubted.

   Therefore the mere absence of any mention of the name of P in the attendance Register would not conclusively prove that he was not an employee of the school.

   (b) Furthermore the possibility that the appellant might have committed a breach of the rules by taking work from the chowkidar at his house instead of sending him to the school cannot be excluded.

   Even if the appellant violated the rules, the charge against him was not that he had violated the rules with a view to causing wrongful loss to the Govt.

   (c) In these circumstances the prosecution case that the appellant had drawn Rs. 50/ and misappropriated the same and made false entries in the accounts, cannot be accepted. Therefore the appellant is acquitted.

S.K. Kale -V- State of Maharastra, A.I.R. 1977 S.C. 822; 1977 Cr. L.J. 604.

The accused, a public servant received monies from P.W.1,

2 and 9 by holding out a promise to them that he will secure some jobs to P.W.'s 2 and 9 in departments other than the Port Trust in which he was employed. It was held that the accused was not abusing his position as a public servant, but was only acting in his individual capacity and that the accused could not be convicted under S. 13 (1) (d) (old Sec. 5 (2)0 read with Sec. 13 (2) (old Sec. 5 (2)) of the Act.

In this case the entire charge against the appellant rests on circumstantial evidence. It was held by the Supreme Court that -

1. Normally, the Supreme Court in Special leave against a concurrent judgement of the High Court and the trial court does not reappraise the evidence, but in this case, both the courts below -
   (a) have drawn wrong inferences from proved facts and
   (b) have made a completely wrong approach to the whole case by misplacing the onus of proof which lay on the prosecution, on the accused.
2. In view of the clear defence taken by the appellant-accused, it was for the prosecution to prove that
   (a) the accused made no enquiries.
   (b) the accused made a departure from the normal procedure with oblique motive and
   (c) the accused knew that the contractor (P.W.2) would make a profit of 45 per cent whereas others would be satisfied with a profit of 10 per cent to 15 per cent.
3. Before a presumption against the accused could be raised that he knew that other firms would have charged a much lesser profit than P.W.2, it should have been proved by the production of account books

of the firms concerned and their dealings during the relevant time that they had sold similar or identical goods and made only a profit of 10 per cent to 15 percent.

> The verbal statements of the witnesses regarding the margin of profit which they would have made had orders been placed 6 years back, can carry no weight.

4. The prosecution has not produced any reliable or conclusive material to prove that the appellant had any dishonest mention in causing pecuniary benefit to P.W.2.

5. Even assuming that the accused departed from the normal procedure in view of the urgent necessity of the articles, it cannot be said that this was done with a corrupt or oblique motive.

   The appellant had been asked by the Dept. to supply these articles immediately. He therefore had to take a quick decision and he was authorised to do so by his chief. Since P.W.2 was prepared to supply all the goods in bulk at one stretch, the appellant may have thought it better to place the orders with him. This may be an error of judgement or an act of indiscretion, but from that alone, an inference of dishonest intention cannot be drawn.

6. Therefore, the prosecution has failed to Drove that the circumstances were such as could be explained only on one hypothesis, namely, that the accused was guilty. The conviction of the appellant is hereby quashed.

Abdulla Mohammed Pagarkar - V- State (Union Territory of Goa), A.I.R. 1980, S.C. 499; 1980 Cr.L.J. 220 (2 judges)

The appellant accused No. 1 who was holding the post

of surveyor in-charge. Mercantile Marine Department and appellant accused No.2 who was working as a contractor, were tried jointly by the Special Judge who found then guilty of offences under -

(a) section 120-B read with section 420, 466 and 471 I.P.C. and

(b) section 5 (1) (d) of the Prevention of Corruption Act, (new section 13).

The prosecution case was that the two appellants entered into a conspiracy to cheat the government in relation to the execution of the work by presenting inflated bills and receiving against them for greater amounts than had actually been spent. The work was to be carried out departmentally. The position which the two appellants took was that the work was being handled directly by the Department and not through any contractor. It was held by the Supreme Court that-

1. There has been no proper approach to the requirements of proof in relation to a criminal charge.

2. The onus of proof of the existence of every ingredient of the charge always rests on the prosecution and never shifts.

   It was therefore incumbents on the State to bring out beyond all reasonable doubt that the number of labourers actually employed in carrying out the work, was less than that stated in the summaries appended to the bills paid for by the Government. It is not safe to rely on the mere impression of the prosecution witnesses about the actual number of labourers employed from time to time.

3. It is very unsafe in the state of the evidence, to agree that the disparity between the estimate arrived at by the prosecution witness and the volume of material

claimed to nave been dredged, proved that the documents on which monies were collected by the accused are false.

In coming to this conclusion, the lower court of judicial Commissioner was also influenced by the factors which raised strong suspicion against the appellant.

4. The findings recorded by the Special Judge and affirmed *by* the judicial Commissioner were correct, but they merely make out that the appellants proceeded to execute the work to flagrant disregard of the relevant Rules of the General Financial Rules and even of ordinary norms of procedural behaviour of govt. officials and contractors in the matter of execution of works, undertaken by the government.

Such discharges, however does not amount to any of the offences of which the appellants have been convicted.

The findings, no doubt, make the suspicion still stronger, but it cannot be said that any of the ingredients of the charge have been made out.

5. Therefore, both the appellant are acquitted of the charges.

Jogeswar Singh Rastogi -v- State of M.P.. A.I.R. 1980; S.C. 366 (2 Judges,); 1979 Cr.App. R. (S.C.) 302; 1980 Gr. L.J. 323

The appellant accused was the Principal of the Institute, and S (P.W.) was the Divisional Forest officer. S wanted to purchase a binocular for the dept. The appellant told S that he had purchased a binocular for his institute and would get the quotations for S also. The appellant gave the binocular (article B) to S. It was not specifically mentioned as to what profit the appellant made in the deal. It was held by the Supreme Court that —

(a) there were differences between Article -A supplied

to the Institute and Article -B supplied to S. It would be hazardous to say that the price paid by *s* was more than the market price.

(b) The prosecution has not succeeded in proving that S was induced to pay higher price then the worth of the article.

(c) Therefore, the offence of cheating has not been established.

(d) The conviction under Sec. 5 (1) (d) of the Act new section 13) is equally unsustainable. The representation that was made by the appellant was as a friend or as a person known to S.

Hemanta Kumar Mohanty -V- State of Orissa 1973 (1) SLR, 112; 1973 (Cut.L.T. 361)

The Orissa High Court disallowed the claim for T.A for tours by car. From the reasoning given by the Judge, it was clear that he would have accepted the claim of the appellant if he would have provided vouchers, cash memos or bills for purchase of petrol, spare parts, garage charges, cooler charges etc. It was held that -

(a) The appellant is to satisfactorily account for the disproportionate assets and not to prove his claim with mathematical exactitude beyond reasonable doubt.

(b) The proper approach to assess the evidence in such cases is to judge the matter on broad probabilities much depending upon the maturity of understanding of the judge. In this case the principles were laid down.

1. T.A. cannot be taken as a legitimate source of income and therefore, onus would not be on the prosecution to lead evidence of the same.

2. Whether savings have been made or not, being with special knowledge of the accused, it is on him to adduce acceptable evidence of the same.
3. If the accused successfully discharges that onus it is not open to the court to brush it aside with the aid of any financial legal fiction.

To sustain a charge under Sec. 5 (e) of the Act (Hew Sec. 13), the prosecution has to show that—

(a) the appellant is/was a public servant.

(b) he himself or on his behalf, someone else -

(i) is possessed or has, at any time during the tenure of his office, been in possession of.

(ii) pecuniary resources disproportionate to his known sources of income for which he could not satisfactorily account.

He cannot expected to keep accounts of expenditure and to procure and preserve supporting bills and vouchers frost the beginning of his career till superannuation.

State of Maharastra -V- Kaliar Koli Subramaniam Ramaswami, A.I.R. 1977; G.C. 2091 (2 Judges), 1977 S.C. Cu. 8. 336; 1977 Cr.L.R. (SC) 372

The respondent accused's house was searched by Inspector on 17.5.64 and a lot of property was recovered from his possession. While the setter was still under investigation, clause (e) was inserted in subsection (1) of Sec. 5 (new section 13) of the Act on 18-12-64, by the Amending Act No. 40 of 1364. A charge sheet was presented in the court of the Special Judge on 3.4.69. The Special Judge convicted the accused for committing offence under clause (e) of sub -section (1) of 3.5 (new Sec. 13). The High Court acquitted him. It was held *by* the Supreme Court -

1. The acquittal of the accused for the offence under clause (e) was justified.
2. In the absence of any evidence on record to show that he acquired, or was found to be in possession of pecuniary resources or property disproportionate to the known sources of income after the coming into force of the Amending Act of 1964, he was entitled to the protection of Art. 20 (1) of the Constitution.
3. It was not permissible for the trial court to convict him of an offence under clause (e) as no such clause was in existence at the relevant time.

Under 3. 5 (1) (e) (new section 13) mere possession of any pecuniary resources or property is not an offence unless

1. the person in possession fails to account satisfactorily of his pecuniary resources or
2. the property in his possession is disproportionate to his known sources of income.

Gauhati High Court Cases

Prabhash Kumar Sen -V- The Criminal Appeal, No. 85 of 1953

(A) Prevention of Corruption Act (IT of 1947) G. 6 - prosecution of Sub— Inspector of Police - S. P. being in full knowledge of the case - sanction accorded by him - validity.

It appears from the evidence of P.W. 4, the Dy. S.P and of P.W.2, the D.C. J.P. Jarman that the J.P, was in the know of things from the beginning. He was a party to laying the trap and he was acquainted with every development in the case and even after the recovery of the marked notes from the possession of the accused, the Dy S.P had contacted the S.P concerned and he stated that after the seizure of articles by the Ext. 10, he produced the accused with the money produced by him before the S.P. and he appraised him of the whole matters and it was after that he submitted this resort Ext. 9 and handed over all the connected papers along-with it. This shows that Mr. Bordoloi was acquainted at that stage with all that had happened and he had given his sanction for prosecution of the accused without anybody else's will being imposed on him.

Held,

> that there may be circumstances when the entire thing may not be known to the sanctioning authority without proper investigation and on these circumstances the sanction may be challenged for being given in insufficient materials. But in this case, so far the S.P. is concerned he must have felt satisfied about the allegations and sanctioned the prosecution unreservedly, So, there was proper sanction for the prosecution of the accused in the present case.

A.I.R. 1953, All. 37, followed A.I.R., 1348, P.C. 82 and A.I.R. 1950, All. 494 approved. (B) Prevention of Corruption Act (II of 1947) -S. 3 Proviso - Investigation. Power of investigation by Inspector of Police as authorised by the D.C. - validity of.

It is not obligatory in all cases that the officer investigating should not be below the rank of the Dy. S.P. and he should not investigate or arrest without the order of the Magistrate of First Class. The proper investigation is that the officer to carry on the investigation or to effect arrest without warrant, if below the rank of the Dy. S.P. should obtain the order of the Magistrate of the First Class to discharge either of these functions, but the Dy. S.P. or any officer above his rank need not obtain such order. In this case, p. Ahmed was an Inspector of Police and he was duly authorised to investigate by the Dy. Commissioner himself. In these circumstances, it cannot be said that the investigation was not proper. Cases referred to:

1. Bharme Sarup -V- the State: A.I.R., 1953, 37.
2. Gokulchand Dawarkdas Morarka - V the King: A.I.R, 1948, P.C. 82.
3. Karim Bux -V- Rex: A.I.R., 1950, 499

Judgement and Order

This is an appeal under S.9 of Act, XLVI of 1952 (Criminal Law Amendment 1952) against the conviction and sentence passed by the Special Judge with respect to an offence tried under Act II of 1947, the Prevention of Corruption Act, 1947. This accused was found guilty under 3.161, I.P.C. and with 3.3 of Act IT of 1947 and was convicted and sentenced to one years rigorous imprisonment and a fine of Rs. 200/ in default to suffer rigorous imprisonment for four months more.

Taking the whole history of the case together, it is beyond doubt that the accused accepted the amount from ram Gobinda with full knowledge as illegal gratification, in this set of circumstances, there is 380 no reason to differ as to the facts of the case from the view taken by the trial court and accordingly affirm the conviction and maintain the substantive term of imprisonment. The fine, however is remitted, with this modification in sentence, the appeal is dismissed.

Sri Nirmalendu Biswas -V- State (Through the Delhi Special Police Establishment), Criminal Appeal No. 92 of 1979: G.L.R. (NOC)5 (1387)2

Prevention of Corruption Act, 1947, 3.6 -Sanction for prosecution - validity of sanction -Sanction granted on 5.7.1975 by the officiating Director of Agriculture whose appointment was quashed by the High Court on 19.5.1978 - judgement of the High Court stayed by the Supreme Court by order dated

14-7-1975 - sanction granted on 5.7.1975 whether valid sanction -Held: No.

S.6 of the Act inter alia - provides that no court shall take cognizance of any offence punishable under S. 161 or 164 or 165 of the I.P.C. or under Subsection (2) orr sub-section (3-A), or S, 5 of the Act, alleged to have been committed by a public servant except with the previous sanction from the authorities mentioned in clauses (a), (b) and (c) of sub-section (l) of the said section 6. Admittedly the accused appellant was a public servant and there is no dispute that the Director of Agriculture, Arunachal Pradesh Administration was the authority competent to remove him from office and as such the sanction for prosecution was to be issued by the said director. The language of S.6 is deer and unambiguous and a valid sanction is a condition precedent to prosecute an accused, who is a public servant in a court of law. Such sanction must be issued by a competent authority as provided in clauses (a), (b) and (c) of the said section. If there is no valid sanction, the condition precedent for taking cognizance of offence by the court is absent, the entire proceeding will be illegal and invalid. On facts Held:

> By an order No. PC 39/65 dated 6.7.73 Sri N. C. Joshi, P.W. 5 was appointed as officiating Director of Agriculture, Arunachal Pradesh administration and this order was challenged before this court by a writ petition which was registered as Civil Rule No. 491 of 1973. By the judgement and order dated 18.5.75, the said notification was quashed. The said judgement of this court was stayed by the Apex Court by an order dt. 14.7.75, passed in Civil Miscellaneous petition No. 3682 of 1975 and the stay order was as follows:
>
> Pending the hearing and final disposal by this court of the said notice of action for stay, the status QUO as

obtaining between the parties herein as on this 14th day of July, 1975 with regard to the post of Director of Agriculture, Arunachal Pradesh shall continue.

Thus it appears that the stay order was operative only from 14th July, 1975 and as such from 19th May, 1975 to 13th July, 1975 Sri Joshi was holding the said post illegally and without due authority. The sanction for prosecution exhibit-120 was issued by Sri Joshi on 5.7.75 that is before the stay order was obtained. As Sri Joshi was molding the post on the date of issuing sanction for prosecution without any authority of law, he was an usurper to the said post and as such the sanction for prosecution, exhibit-120 accorded by the P.W.5 on 5.7.75 is a nullity. In view of the above legal position the doctrine of De facto' will not be applicable, in respect of the said sanction order, exhibit-120. It is therefore held that there was no valid and legal sanction for prosecution in the instant case and as such the condition precedent for taking cognizance of the case by the trial court was absent. On this ground alone the trial and the impunged judgement and order are liable to be quashed.

Debendra Singh -V- The State of Assam Criminal Appeal, No. 24 of 1977: G.L.R. 66 (1983)1

Prevention of Corruption Act, 1947 - S.5 A and 6 - sanction for prosecution.

S.5 A does not contemplate two sanctions one for laying a trap and another for further investigation. Once an order underv that provision is made, that order covers the entire investigation.

Prevention of Corruption Act, 1947 - S.6. Sanction necessary for prosecution under S.6 of the Act, for charges under 3. 5 (2) reed with S. 165 of I.P.C. It should be clean from the sanction itself that the sanctioning authority considered the evidence before it and after a consideration of all the circumstances of the prosecution and therefore, unless the mutter can be proved by other evidence, in the sanction itself, the fact should be conferred to indicate that the sanctioning authority had applied its mind to the facts and circumstances of the case.

On the facts of the case,

> held - In face of evidence on record it will not be safe to held that the sanctioning authority did not apply his mind while according the sanction for prosecution. The sanction was in accordance with law.

Evidence Act, 1872, S. 3 - Interested witnees-Witnesses concerned in the success of the trap- whether interested witnesses. Held:

> In the instant case, though the prosecution witnesses may perhaps be called interested witnesses in the sense they were concerned in success of trap, they cannot be called interested witnesses in the sense that they were out to procure conviction of the appellant. Cases referred Chronological
>
> Prakash Chand -V- State (Delhi Administration), A.I.R. 1979 S.C. 400.
>
> Raghbir Singh -V- State of Punjab
>
> Nanak Chand -V- State of Himchal Pradesh; A.I.R. 1974 Cr.L.J. 606.
>
> Om Prakash -V- State of Delhi A.I.R. S.C. 989. Ram prakash Arora -V- state of Punjab; A.I.R. 1973; G.C. 498.

Order

On consideration of relevant papers sanction accorded to prosecution of Sri D.C. Singh Deben Singha, LDA Land acquisition Branch of D.C Office Silcher in connection with Silcher P.S. case P.S. case No. 40 (II) 75 under S. 165, I.P.C. read with 3.5 (2) of Prevention of Corruption Act, in the court of law under Provision of S. 6 of P.C. Act, (Act No. 2) of 1947.

Considering the entire facts and circumstances of the case, no infirmity was found in the impunged judgement of conviction. Also there is no reason to interfere with the sentence. The appeal is accordingly rejected. The appellant is on bail. He is to surrender forthwith to serve out the remaining part of the sentence, subject to set off under 3. 428 Cr.P.C.

The State of Assam -V- Reba Nath Bhattacharyya, (1986) 2 GLR 70: Criminal Revision No. 128 of 1976 Decided on 24.1.1986

Prevention of Corruption Act, 1947, Ss.5 (1) (d) and 5 (2) - I.P.C., S. 120-B - Offence under - Nature of - in order to come within the purview of S.5 (l) (d), the abuse of the position must necessarily be dishonest so that it may be proved that the accused caused deliberate loss to the Department - Acts of irregularity, carelessness or rushness unless tainted with dishonest intention cannot amount to criminal misconduct within the meaning of S. 5 (l) (d) of the Act. Cases referred: Chronological:

> S.P. Bhatnagar -V- State of Maharashtra (1979) 1 SCC 535 Major S.K. Kale -V- State of Maharastra; A.I.R. 1977 SC 822 State of Karnataka. -V- Maniswami and others, A.I.R. 1977) S.C. 822
>
> M. Narayanan Namibiar -V- State of Kerela, A.I.R. 1963 S.C. 1116
>
> Dhaneswar Karain Saxena -V- the Delhi Administration, A.I.R. 1962; S.C. 195

Judgement and Order (Oral)

Das J - We are not at all convinced *by* the strenuous

argument of Mr. C.R.D, learned Public Prosecutor that it is a fit case where the provision of S.5 (l) (d) read with S.5 (2) of the P.C. Act is attracted. The learned Special Judge before whom the trial proceeded had rightly come to the conclusion that the trial was not within the jurisdiction of the learned spacial Judge as because these were no prima facie material to show that the accused person could be tried. S.5 (1) (d) read with S.5 (2) of the P.C. Act and S. 120 E of the I.P.C. The four accused persons against whom offence report was submitted under S. 420/468/477 A/409 I.P.C reed with S.5 (2) of the P.C. Act read with S. 109 of the I.P.C. were sent up for trial before the learned Special Judge, Assam at Gauhati. The learned Judge considered all the materials on record which were made available before him and found that there was no prima facie case against the opposite party No. 1 to frame charge under 3.5 (2) read with;. 5 (l) (d) of the.. .. Act and under S. 123 5 of the I.P.C,. Therefore the learned Judge who was empowered to try the offence under S.6 of the Criminal Law (Amendment) Act, found that it was not within the jurisdiction of the learned Judge to try the case against the opposite parties under the provision of Law. The learned Judge further held that, as the case was not covered by those materials to be tried by the Special judge having no jurisdiction to try the same, the offence alleged to have been committed by the accused could be tried by the Court of ordinary jurisdiction and on that finding, the learned Judge declined to proceed further with the case.

2. We have learned Mr. C.R. De, learned Public Prosecutor at length as well as Mr. J.P Bhattacharyya, learned counsel appearing on behalf of the opposite party No. 1, Mr. S. Medhi appearing for the opposite party No. 2 and Mr. M.A.L. Laskar, Mr. Sulaiman, learned counsel on behalf of the opposite party No. 3 and 4. The learned Public Prosecutor has lead to the impunged order and have found that, the learned Judge

while considering the material evidence on record found that the facts did not indicate dishonest mind of accused R.N. Bhattacharyya. It might be an act of irregularity, carelessness or rashnees. But in a criminal charge if there is no material to show that the act of the accused was tainted with dishonest intention, it cannot amount to criminal misconduct within the meaning of S.5 (l) (d) of the P.C. Act, unless a corrupt practice is illegally adopted to abuse the official position. The learned Judge found that there was no such dishonest intention appearing in the case against the accused R.N. Bhattacharyya to come to the conclusion that offence under S. 5 (2) read with S.5 (l) (d) of the P.C. Act and under 120 B of the I.P.C. to rope the accused persons in the trial. Reliance is sought to be pieced by Mr. C.R. De, learned public Prosecutor on two decisions of their Lordship of the Supreme Court as reported in A.I.R 1962, S.C. 13S (Dhaneswar Narain Saxena -V- The Delhi Administration) and A.I.R. 1963 S.C.1116 (M. Narayan Namibiar -V State of Kerela). There cannot be, any dispute as to the pro-position of law laid down by their lordship in catena of case of like nature relating to the offence punishable under S.5 (2) of the P.C. Act, read with S. 120 B and G. 109 of I.P.C, In S.P, Bhatnagar -V- State of Maharashtra as reported in (1973)1 3CC 535 under Lordship held that S.5 (l) (d) of the P.C Act requires that the abuse of the position. In order to come within the mischief of this section must necessarily be dishonest so that it may be proved that the accused caused deliberate loss to the Department. Also it is for the prosecution to prove affirmatively that the accused by corrupt or illegal means or by abusing his position obtained any pecuniary advantage for some other person. Therefore the question *in* this case arises as to whether the first accused obtained pecuniary advantage either for himself or for some other person by adopting corrupt or illegal means or by abusing his position of the office with dishonest intention. In the present case after going through the documents, the learned Judge found that the facts revealed could not show that the accused No. 1 acted with dishonest intention and that other material ingredients were available to frame a charge under S.5 (2; read with S. 5 (l) (d) of P.C. Act and under S.120 B read with S.109 I.P.C. The opposite party No. 1 (first accused) filed an affidavit in opposition in this case. Alongwith affidavit *in* opposition he has produced certain documents which were very much available before the learned special Judge. It appears that the accused No. 1 acted at the direction of S.D.O. (civil), Nalbari. The learned Special Judge also found that the materials available were not sufficient to rope the accused with charge under S.5 (1) (d) and S.120 B of the I.P.C. We have also found that the learned Special Judge correctly held that there was no sufficient ground for proceeding against the accused No. 1 along with others under S.5 (2) read with S.5 (1) (d) of P.C. Act and under. 120 s read with S 108 of I.P.C.

3. As regards dishonest intention Mr. J.P. Bhattacharyya, learned counsel appearing on, behalf of accused No. 1 has drawn our attention to the decision of their Lordship of the S.S. in A.I.R. 1977, S.C. 822 (Major S.K. Kale -V- State of Maharastra), A.I.R. 1977, S.C. 1489 (State of Karnataka - V- L. Kunisawmi and others) and (1979)1 SCC 535 (S.P. Bhathnagar- v - state of Maharastra) There cannot be early dispute on the principles as laid down by their lordship of the S.C. in this regard, on going through the materials on record before us we do not find any reason for our interference with impunged order passed by the learned special Judge. The petition is accordingly being meritorious.

Sudhendra Kumar Bhattacharyya -V - State (Delhi Special Police Establishment), (1967)1 GLR, 80.

Prevention of corruption Act, 1947, Ss 5 (2) read with S (1) (c) - Appellant prosecuted under S.5 (2) read with S.5(l) (c) of the Act and S. 409 of the I.P.C.-Sanction accorded for prosecution of the appellant invalid infirmity in sanction whether effected trial under S. 409 of I.P.C. Held - Yes

The salutary requirement of obtaining previous sanction as required by S.6 of the Act cannot be set at naught by prosecuting a public servant for an offence under the penal Code for which no sanction is necessary though the offence attracts the mischief of the provision (5) of law mentioned in S.6 of the Act. Such a course would really frustrate *the* purpose for which previous sanction has been deemed necessary by the legislature.

On facts held:- The allegations in the present case admittedly falling within the mischief of S.5 (2) of the Act and S. 409 of the Penal Code, no prosecution could have been launched against the appellant only under S. 409 of the Penal Code. Now if he could not have been put up for trial under S. 409, there can be no dispute that he could not have been found guilty under S. 409 at the conclusive decision of the trial. The conviction of the appellant under S. 409 cannot therefore be mentioned, as the trial for the offence alone has to be regarded as without Jurisdiction and as such nonest in the eye of law.

Cases referred: Chronological:

A. Verraih -V- State, A.I.R. 1957. A.P. 663.

K.P. Sinha -v- Atabuddin, A.I.R., 1955; Pat. 453

Om Prakash -V- Emperor, A.I.R. 1939 P.C. 43.

Mohammed Abdul Salman -V- State of Assam, (1988) 2 (HOC) 33

Section 5 (2) - Special reasons for purpose of awarding lesser sentence than the minimum prescribed-Special reasons for the purpose of awarding lesser sentence than the minibus prescribed means special to the accused to whom sentence is being imposed - Factors constituting special reasons' for mitigating remitting the sentences stated. Held,

Special reasons in the proviso of section 5 (2) of the P.C, Act, for the purpose of awarding lesser sentence than that of minimum prescribed, means 'special' to the accused on whom sentence is being imposed. Accused appellant Abdul Salem was under suspension from 24.5.1957 and finally lost his job with heart, having dependents consisting of four school/ College going children besides a wife, also suffering from Hypertension and Insomnia since 1980 which deteriorated health; had central tension and agony during 22 years of trial/appeal period causing sufference unimaginable in volume; all those years he travelled from his home (Dibrugarh) to the place of trial (Gauhati) for this litigation that crippled his financial/economic status beside huge litigation expenses, undue delay in trial/ appeal for 22 years kept him hanging with uncertainty in life. All these collectively constitute 'special' reasons for mitigating/remitting the sentences. If is fit case for remission of the sentence.

Ved Prakash Goel -V- P. Banie, S.P. C.M's Vigilence Cell, Dispur, (1963) 1 GLR (NOC)17

Section 5 (1) (c) - Public servant causing loss to government by undervalueing timber and issuing permits to non-existent firms whether liable under S.5 (l) (c). Held:

> If the public servant in this case caused loss to the government by undervalueing timber and issuing permit to non-existent firms, the public servant could be liable.
>
> Maxim - Quod initio non valet, tractum temporis does not become valid by lapse of time, on facts held that materials collected in course of investigation pursuant to FIR lodged in bed faith cannot cure the initial bad faith

Prafulla Chandra Mech -V- Delhi Special Police Establishment C.I.A. (II), New Delhi, (1391) 2 GLR 170

Criminal Revision No 202 of 1981 decided on 28.11.1990.

Prevention of Corruption Act, 1947 -whether applicable in Jowai in Meghalaya held: Yes.

By notification dt. 8.5.1947, and 19.5.1947 the P.C. Act 1947 was made applicable to the "excluded areas" and "partially excluded areas" of the state of Assam. Jowai is within the "partially excluded " areas. In such view of the matter, the Act was brought into operation in Jowai from 1947 by the exercise of authority by the Governor.

The position has not changed after commencement of the Constitution and it continues to be in force.

Delhi Special Police Establishment Act, 1946—whether applicable to Jowai in Meghalaya- held: Yes.

Constitution of India, Article 21 - Undue delay in trial- occurrence took place, between April, 1970 and December, 1970 - Charge sheet submitted in 1947 - Case pending since then for no fault of the accused - considering the overall circumstances of the case, trial -prosecution of the accused closed by the High Court.

Judgement

The revision petition arises from an order of the Special Judge, Shillong in Special Case No. 36 of 1947/2 of 1979 made on 12.5 81.

2. Facts - The accused Prafulla Chandra Mech, the petitioner herein was working as Executive Engineer, Jowai, Bedarpur Road Construction Division. Government of Assam from April, 1970 to December, 1971. The accusation against him was that during the said period of 20 months, the income of the accused from different known sources was Rs. 82,

668.85. His expenditure during the said 20 months was Rs. 43, 554.63. On an enquiry, it was found that luring the said period of 20 months, assets of the petitioner in hand was Rs. 1,02, 209.00 and therefore, he was found possessing assets disproportions to the known sources of income, viz., Rs. 66,094. 88 (after giving margin). The accused petitioner as a public servant has thus committed offence punishable under section 5 (2) read with 5 (1) (c) of the P.C. Act, 1947. On the basic of an FIR dt. 18.2.74, the Delhi Special Police Establishment investigated the offence and submitted charge-sheet dt. 31.11.74.

3. After submission of the charge-sheet, the petitioner has challenged the jurisdiction of the Delhi Special Police Establishment to investigate the offence alleged to have been committed by him at Jowai and to submit charge-sheet. The learned Special Judge has held that the Delhi Special Police Establishment had Jurisdiction to investigate the offence, hence this petition.

4. Mr. D.K. Bhattacharyya, the learned counsel for the petitioner has advanced two submissions. First the P.C. Act, 1947, for short" the Act of 1947", has not been extended to Jowai where the occurrence took place, Secondly, the Govt. of India has not extended the powers and jurisdiction of the members of the Delhi special Police Establishment under S. 5 read with S.6 of the Delhi Special Police Establishment Act, 1946, for short" the Act of 1946" in Jowai.

5. Before the commencement of the Constitution of India under S. 92 of the Government of India Act, 1935, for *short* "the Act of 1965", no Act of the federal Legislature, or of the Provincial Legislature shall apply to an excluded areas the partially excluded area, unless the governor *by* public notification so directs. section 91 of the Act of 1935 defines excluded areas and partially excluded areas. Under S. 91 of

the Act of 1935 the expression "excluded areas" and "partially excluded areas" mean respectively such areas as His Majority may by order in council declare to be excluded areas or partially excluded areas. On March 3, 1936, the Government of India (Excluded and Partially Excluded Areas), order, 1935, for short "the order" was issued under the order in the State of Assam 'excluded' areas were and/or are the North East Frontier (Sadiya, Balipara and Lakhimpur) Tracts the Naga Hills District, the Lushai Hills district and the North Cachar Hills Sub-Division of the Cacher District and the partially excluded areas were and/or are the Garo Hills District the Mikir Hills (in the Nowgong and Sibsagar District) and the British portion of the Khasi and Jaintia Hills District, other than the Shillong Municipality and Cantonment.

After the formation of the State of Meghalya it appears that with regard to the Act of 1946. The Act of 1947 and the regulation, no adaptation has been made, by the reason of the absence of adaptation by the Government of Meghalya, it cannot be said that the Acts and regulations passed by the Government lapsed for the reason that operation of the existing laws is not conditioned by making adaptation and notifications by the Government. For all such reasons, the Act of 1946 was brought into application by legislative enactment on and from 26 January, 1950 and the Act 1947 was extended and continues to be in force, in the State including Jowai where the occurrence took place.

The next question which arises for consideration is whether the case shall be sent back for consideration of the charge. The Constitutional position is now well settled that the right to a speedy trial is one of the dimensions of the fundamental rights to life and liberty guaranteed by Article 21 of the Constitution, that is to say, speedy trial is a fundamental right implicit in the guarantee of life and personal liberty enshrined in Article 21 of the Constitution far "fair and reasonable procedure" is what is contemplated by the expression "procedure established by law " under Art. 21. Therefore, the infringement to the right in appropriate cases would be sufficient to quash conviction or stop further proceedings. What is the appropriate case is the question. It depends upon the variety of relevant factors.

Coming to the case on hand, the occurrence place between April 1970 and December 1971. The first information report was lodged on 18.2.74. The charge-sheet was submitted on 31.12.74. The case has been pending from 1974 till date for no fault of the accused. There has been enormous delay and the sword has been hanging over the head of the accused for the last more than 16 years. It is true that offences of that kind should not be allowed to go unpunished. But, as already stated, quick justice is sine quo non of the Art. 21 of the Constitution of India. Considering the overall circumstances of the case, it would be just and fair to direct that the trial or prosecution of the petitioner to proceed no further. In the result, the proceeding against the petitioner are quashed. The petitioner is allowed.

Discussion on Judicial Findings

The question of corruption in public life is very important as is evident from the number of cases and the variety of causes involved as can be gauged from the reports of the cases of the High Courts as well as the Supreme Court of India. Rampant corruption in all walks of life has been adequately substantiated by the courts in India. It is evident from the decisions of the Supreme Court and High Courts in India that the existing provisions of Sec. 6 (new Sec. 19) of the prevention of Corruption Act, 1947, regarding obtaining' of previous sanction necessary for prosecution of a Government or public servant often leads to failure. Sec. 6 of the Act inter alia provides that no court shall take cognizance of any offence punishable under Sec, 161 or Sec. 164 or Sec. 165 of the

Indian penal Code, 1860 or under sub-section (2) or sub-section (3-A) or Sec. 5 of the Prevention of Corruption Act, 1947 alleged to have been committed by Government or public servant except with the previous sanction from the authorities mentioned in clauses (a), (b) and (c) or sub-section (1) of the said Sec. 6. Since a valid sanction is a condition precedent to prosecute an accused who is also a public servant in a court of law, there appears to be enough escape route for such a corrupt public servant from the legal net, because of inconsistencies leading to invalid sanction for prosecution (Sri Nirmalendu Biswas -V- State: Through the Delhi Special police Establishment; Cr. Appeal No. 92 of 1979).

It can be gathered from the judicial pronouncements in many cases, that the prosecution of most corrupt public servant may fail owing to procedural wranglings or cobwebs resulting from patent lapses of executives assessed Under Sec 161 or Sec. 164 or Sec. 165 of the Indian Penal Code, 1860 or under sub-section (2) or sub-section (3-A) of Sec. 5 of the prevention of Corruption Act, 1947. The recent Antulay case filed before the Bombay high Court is a happy exception in this respect. Many other litigations decided by the supreme Court and High Courts in India highlight the deficiencies in the existing provisions of granting previous sanction for prosecution. It was held in R.S. Noyak -V- A.R. Antulay, that where offences as set out in Sec. 6 are allowed to have been committed by a public servants, sanction of only that authority would be necessary which would be competent to remove him from that office. In the instant case, the court could not take cognizance of the offence due to lack of a valid sanction for prosecution. In R. Menon -V - Union of India, 1966 (c) 387, where the accused ceased to be a public servant at the time, the court took cognizance of offence. It was decided that the Sec. 6 of the Act, does not apply. In Dharmadatan, K.S. -V- Central Government, A.I.R. 1979, it was held by the Supreme

Court that, Sec. 19 (old Sec. 6) of the prevention of Corruption Act, applies only where at the time when the offence was committed, the offender was acting as a public servant. As the appellant in this case had ceased to be a public servant at the time when the cognizance of the case was taken against him by the Special Judge, no sanction under Sec. 19 (old Sec. 6) was necessary. Similarly in State - V -Banshilal Luhadlay, A.I.R. 1982, Rajasthan 250; S. A. Venkataraman -V- State, A.I.R., 1968, S.C. 107, the Supreme Court could not take cognizance of the offence because the accused ceased to be a public servant at the time when the cognizance of the offence was taken. The above account definitely points out the lacunae of the Act, causing miscarriage of justice in taking the cognisance of the offence. A systematic and thorough review of the laws, rules, procedures and practices should be undertaken with a view to removing the existing lacunae in the scheme of litigation to fight corruption. These loopholes are often found to widen themselves into thorough fares through which corrupt officials defeat the purpose of law.

Sec. 4 (1) of the Prevention of Corruption Act, requires the presumption to be raised whenever it is proved that an accused person has accepted any illegal gratification (other than legal remuneration) or any valuable thing. The presumption raised by Sec. 4 has to be rebutted by proof and not by mere explanation which may be simply plausible. The operation of Sec. 4 (l) is confined to a trial of an offence punishable under Sec. 161 or Sec. 165 of the I.P.C. or under clause (a) or (b) of Sec. 5 (1) read with sub-section (2) of that section of the prevention of Corruption Act. The verdict of the Supreme Court in R.S. Nayak -V- A.R. Antulay (1986) 2 S.C.C. 716, 722, 723, 1986, S.C.C. (Cri) 256 was that - presumption under Sec. 4 of the prevention of Corruption Act (Sec. 20 of new Act) to be taken into account both when the court considers whether charge should be framed or not as well us after the framing of the charge. Similarly in Dhanavantrai -V- State of Maharashtra, A.I.R. 1964, S.C. 575, it was held by the supreme Court that unless the explanation is supported by proof, the presumption created by the provision cannot be said to be rebutted. It further held that the question, whether a presumption of law or fact stands rebutted by evidence or other material on record, is one of fact and not of law. The decisions of the cases triad under Sec. 4 of the Prevention of Corruption Act, indicates that the existing provisions of Sec. 4 of the Act have some deficiencies causing failure in prosecution. Other important cases tried under Sec. 4 of the Act are - state of Madras - V -A. Vaidyanatha Iyer, A.I.R. 1958, S.C. 61; V.D. Jhingam -V- State of U.P., A.I.R. 1068, S.C. 1762, 1966; State of Assam -V- Krishna Rao and another, A.I.R., 1973, S.C. 28; State of Rajasthan -V- Mohammad Habib, A.I.R 1973, Cr.L.J. 703; Bhupesh Deb Gupta -V- State of Tripura, A.I.R. 1978, S.C. 1673, Cr.L.J. 1738; Banshilal -V- State of Bihar, A.I.R. 1981, S.C. 1235, 1981, Cr.L.J. 741, 1381; pandurang Laxman -V- State of Bombay, A.I.R,, 1959, Allahabad 483,; Jaswant Singh -V- State of Punjab, A.I.R. 1973, S.C. 707, 1973; Kunhi Mohammed -V- State, A.I.R. 1959, Kerela 88.

It is noticeable from the findings of many litigations in court cases against bribery and corruption that it becomes very difficult to establish cases of accepting illegal gratification by a public servant, though the ramifications of this serious type of offence is very wide in public life. One of the loopholes of the provisions under Sec. 4 of the Act, may be that the Sec. does not provide for punishment of the bribe giver. The section is applied only when it is established that the accused received gratification in the form of consideration as a motive or reward which was not legal. It will be more effective, if the Sec. provides punishment to both the parties thereto and the abettors on either side if any. Sec. 5 (l) (d) of the prevention of Corruption Act, 1947 relates to misconduct by a public servant by corrupt or illegal means or otherwise and obtaining pecuniary advantage for himself or the others in whom he is vitally interested. The effectiveness of this provision has been somewhat blinted by the its and buts contained in the judicial pronouncements. In order to make the original intention of the legislature, crystal clear, clause 13 (1) (d) has been split into three parts. Further, a definition of the expression "known sources of income" has been added to remove any ambiguity, Sec. 5 of the Prevention and Corruption Act, created the offence of criminal misconduct on the part of the public servant, an offence unknown in connection with the interpretation of any of the provisions of the I.P.C. dealing with illegal gratification like bribery or corruption. The provisions of Sec. 5 under clauses (a), (b), (c) and (d) supposed to be more effective for combating corruption of public servants. If a man obtains a pecuniary advantage by the abuse of his position, he will be guilty under clause (d). Sec. 161, Sec. 162 and Sec. 163 refer to a motive or reward for doing or forebearing to do something, showing favour or disfavour to any person or for such misconduct by the exercise of personal influence. It is not necessary for an offence under clause (d) to prove all these. It is enough if by abusing the position as a public servant, a man obtains for himself any pecuniary advantage entirely irrespective of motive or reward for showing favour or disfavour.

The Supreme Court has confirmed in Ram Krishna- V - State of Delhi, A.I.R., 1956, S.C. 476, 1956, S.C.R. 182,1958; S.A. Venkataraman -V- The State, A.I.R. 1958, S.C. 107, 1958; Dhanavantrai Bawantrai - V — State of Maharastra, A.I.R., 1964, S.C. 575; Deonath Dudhnath Mishra -V- State of Maharastra, A.I.R., 1967, Bombay Ram Dulare Yadav -V- State of U.P., Cr.L.J. 933 (Allahabad) 1971; Dalpat Singh -V- State of Rajasthan, A.I.R. 1969, S.C. 17,1969, Cr.L.J. 363 (1968);

Maha Singh -V- State (Delhi Administration), A.I.R. 1978, S.C. 449, 1978, Cr.L.J. 348 (1978); R.C. Jacob - V -Republic of India, A.I.R. 1963, S.C. 550,1963 (3) S.C.R. 600 (1963); S.K. Kale -V- State of Maharastra A.I.R 1977, S.C. 822, Cr.L.J. 604, 1977; Abdulla Mohammad Pagarkar -V- State (Union Territory of Goa), A.I.R., 1980, Cr.L.J. 220; jogeswar Singh Rastogi -V- State of M.P., A.I.R. 1980, S.C. 366) Hemanta Kumar Mohanty -V- State of Orissa, 1973 (1) SIR 112; State of Maharashtra -V- Kaliar Koil, S. Ramaswami, A.I.R. 1077, S.C. 2091.

Though such provisions of the prevention of Corruption Act, are supposed to be most effective in combating corruption of public servants, in practice the problem instead of reducing its dimension has widened it in an unlimited manner. Since it has its roots and ramifications in society as a whole, every culture has to devise its own remedy depending on the depth and spread of the tentacles or the roots. Effective provisions of anti-corruption laws to tackle the problem not only of public servants but also of Ministers, M.P.'s and M.L.A.s are required to be devised. Recent unhappy trends in many countries especially in Japan or in Italy have proved that corruption in public places has almost become common. These trends must be arrested by all kinds of efforts, be it through legislation or other means of social awareness. Otherwise there will eat into the vitals of morality and development in the country.

SOME MAJOR SCAMS

1. Political Scam

Political entrepreneur flourish or perish according to the quantities of public resources they control and the way they use their resources. Yet the patron has always to maintain the edge between possession and expenditure of the resources they control. The politicians in power give away the resources more in the form of personalised favour than conserve it. It is the duty of the political entrepreneur to divert the flow of resources from State agencies to private citizens.

India is on the threshold of completing fifty years of national freedom. There has been during these long period of independence, significant national material progress in the country. But the expectation from freedom demolished ultimately causing in total failure to create a sound economic health an effective social system and a classless society. There was a divergence between the provision of material goods and the effort for nation building. The divergence has increased with time, Thus there is serious concern with the leadership, the Indian political system has been able to generate and its performance. The promises of leaders were targetted at special interest rather than the general messes. There are lives full of depravity, discrimination, deprivation and perpetual uncertainty in the one hand and doubts about honesty and credibility of the government on the other.

The Home Minister comrade Indrajit Gupta, on his first visit after taking oath to Calcutta called for a national campaign against corruption. In his opinion one should proceed in the matter by setting up citizens committee. On the same day T.N. Seshan, the Chief Election Commissioner appealed at a meeting of big industrialists in Calcutta for launching the second phase of our freedom struggle with the objective of eradicating corruption. Political leaders both at the centre as well as in States since independence categorically speaking of waging struggle against corruption. The former Prime Minister Deve Gowda too has announced his government's firm position against corruption and criminalisation. India is now ranks among most corrupt countries of the world, we are in the same category as Argentina, Brazil, South Korea, The Philipines. A country where honesty and morality of the Ministers, M.P.s, M.L.A.s and Bureaucrats are in question, all the misdeeds and corruption are not pathetic consequence, but natural for that country. It is quite unfortunate that a former Prime Minister has to approach the court to exempt him from personally appearing in a case involving Section 420 of the Cr.P.C. where necessary investigations are not conducted into the repeated allegations of violation of law by the family members of the same personality. The countless erstwhile Ministers are charged with having earned money through unfair means. Had the erstwhile leaders, executives and other personalities in power and privilege in Independent India were free from corruption and sincere in preserving morality and justice and honesty, the country would not destroy and lead to such a pathetic position.

The incidence of corruption has spread everywhere. It has affected everyone, almost all parties by and large. Violation of law and misuse of power are the source of corruption. Accepting money in exchange of granting the advantage, inaction in investigation, disorderly conduct of trial are some of the antisocial activities practised by dishonest personalities in politics enjoying power and privileges. Another great advantage granted to those personalities directly or indirectly by the statute is that persons enjoying power and self do not have to answer for their misdeeds. Corruption in our country has turned into a norm of life and one has got accustomed to the situation, The most alarming situation prevalent in this time is the people's lack of confidence. No political party in India could succeed in creating a new society free from corruption, injustice, division of class, caste and religion. The causes of failure are manifold. However at least one of the reasons is alround corruption and misuse of power. The honest leaders and workers, the common people must have protested the corrupt activities of dishonest leaders. But they could not collectively prevent the party's decay due collapse of internal legal framework of the party. Unfortunately the political parties of our country even the leftist have failed to draw the lessons of consequences of the past. The Congress governments have already lost their credibility having been listed the leaders one after another as accused in financial scams.

The bribes offered by the Bofors Company of Sweden do get a defence contract was accented by the Ministry. The Harshad Mehta, the Hitens, the Krishnamurthy, the Venkataramanas and the Ambanis looted at least Rs. 10,000 crores through forgeries with political indulgence. The international sugar barons secured additional profits through advance information of imports from Kalpanath Rai, the then Union Minister. In return the Ministers and Bureaucrats collected handsome money for their individual profit. With a view to fulfilling the motive of earning money through supply of equipments by a Hyderabad -based firm, despite the fact that it had furnished highest price quotation, Sukh Ram removed the honest officials and posted his own men and women in their places. Crores of rupees earned in the process. In all these processes of looting money, the Ministers, the Bureaucrats and Businessmen are involved.

The States also are not lagging behind and staggering corruption paralally with the Central Ministers. LOC scam of Rs. 200 crores in Assam, T.V. sets purchase at the highest price lossing Rs 8.53 crores by the Chief Minister of Tamil Nadu, J. Jaylalitha, Enrom Project case of Maharastra involving roughly $ 30 billion over the span of 20 years agreement, the Fodder scam of Bihar government headed by Laloo Prasad Yadav are a few of the severe corruption cases detected in States. However it is good sign for us that the courts fight political corruption during 1996 as never before. The Supreme Court, Delhi High Court and lower court Judges and lawyers while attending the Golden Jubilee celebration of the constitution of Constituent Assembly at Vigyan Bhavan at New Delhi expressed their valuable remarks in unusually good spirits against political corruption. In the same function, the President of India, Dr Sankar Dayal Sharma said that, in a climate in which most politicians would like to curtail the power of judges, there was at least one man at the top who could be expected to resist the attempts to straitjacket them. The Chief Metropolitan magistrate Prem Kumar said, while trying the Lakhubhai Pathak case, "Various scams show the unholy nexus of politicians, power brokers, bureaucrats and businessmen in debasing and devalueing the moral authority of our political system. But time is no respect of persons. The basic tenet of the rule of law is: be you ever so high, the law is above you". During the year 1996 alone a good number of corruption cases of top politicians in power tried abiding by the status and position of judiciary. The important corruption cases against which trials are initiated during the year are - Urea scandal involving 1.33 crores of the former Union Minister Ram Lakhan Yadav, Illegal allotment of 2000 government houses by Sheila Kaul and P.K. Thangoon- former Ministers of Urban development, Hawala cases of receiving Hawla money from the industrialist S.K. Jain by a good number of Narashimha Rao government, JMM case involving some Union Ministers of Narasimha Rao government, Lakhubhai Pathak case involving the Prime Minister himself and others transacting illegal money of $100000 through the Godman Chandraswami, St. KITTS Affair of the central government.

It is a matter of regret that the Prevention of Corruption Act does not cover the corrupt politicians. By exclusions of corrupt politicians from the purview of the Prevention of Corruption Act indirectly gives free hand to corrupt politicians to do corrupt practices for personal gain. Last fortnight, M.P.s of most political parties wished not to be termed public servant, because it brings them under the purview of the PC Act. A senior judge of the Supreme Court said - " This is the only way left for them to legalise their looting". Politicians need money for promoting themselves in politics, businessmen need the patronage of personal in the government to become millionaire easily and quickly by offering hard cash and other services to them. In the system both patronise criminals to get the unlawful things done smoothly. This nexus is an open secret.

Corruption no doubt a global phenomenon, but all existing systems have adaptability to weed it out. But the Indian democracy is inapt to respond quickly to scams and the caucuses which protect such practices. Many Prime ministers in Japan resigned because of their involvement in bribery scandals, the U.S. President had resigned for their involvement in the Water Gate scandal. But India is not included in such list, The Indian democracy is indebted to the independent judiciary which has passed judgements related to Lakhubhai Pathak cheating case, Jharkhand Mukti Morcha M.P.s pay off, St. Kitts conspiracy, ARMS Telecom scandal.

The scams of the recent past have significant contributions towards rapid deterioration of economic health of the country as a whole. The scams involving more than crores of rupees are-

Bank Security Scam	Rs. 7000 crores
Hawla Scam	Rs. 65 crores
Animal Husbandry Scam	Rs. 950 crores
Urea Scam	Rs. 133 crores
Sugar Scam	Rs. 600 crores
Air Bus Scam	Rs. 1200 crores
Medical Equipment Scam	Rs. 1000 crores
ARMS Telecom Scam	Rs. 1.6 crores

Misuse of power for corruption is a common phenomenon

among the people having power to deal with resources and money. Absolute power corrupt absolutely. In order to check corruption effectively, much remains to be done positively and constructively. Amendments of relevant provisions in the Prevention of Corruption Act so as to bring the corrupt politicians to the legal net is one of the essential steps of positive action. Boycott of corrupt politicians and officials from the society, imposing restrictions in election, introduction of code of conduct for politicians are some other steps required for control of corruption at least to a significant extent if not completely.

In the Heritage corridor Scam of 175 Crores the C.M. of U.P and seven others were charged by the C.B.I. in October, 2003. Following directions of the Apex Court. The other accused in the case are Mayawatis party colleague and former Environment Minister of U.P., Nisimuddin Siddique and battery of U.P.'s top bureaucrat's including former chief Secretary of U.P., D.S Bagga, P.L. Punia who served as Principal Secretary to Mayawati and R.K. Sharma, the State's Environment Secretary Mayawati who also implicated for the disproportionate assets after this Taj Corridor scam. She had properties worth crores of rupees in different town of U.P. in the name of her brothers, cousins and other relatives. In the Stamp paper Scam jake stamp papers were printed and circulated in the market by one abdul Karim Telgi and his associates with the patronage of Political bigwigs and senior Police officials. This scam has broken all the records involving the approximate amount of As. 31,000 crores.

These political corruptions are some not of Most scams which could not be unearthed.

2. Bureaucratic Corruption

Bureaucratic corruption is as old as government office, We hear of it in Babylon and in Rome, in Classical India of the third country B.C. and in many other countries. In the modern era it appears in all the worlds and in all spheres of life, corruption is perennial and ubiquitous to be found in any and all systems of government. She problems is therefore is not to account for its presence, but rather for its existence and extent. Use of public power for private advantage is a serious offence and the public servants exercising such power in illegal acts are the society's No. 1 enemy, because of the injury to the public interest. In India the personalities of civil services are exercising key powers of the public offices and as such detachment of the acts done by Ministries on the one and subordinate officers on the other end is not possible,. Under many circumstances of illegalities and corruption, nexus between civil servants and politicians or civil servants and their subordinates or businessmen politicians to be present.

Study of several instances of corruption from time to time including the study conducted by the Santhanam Committee in independent India suggests that three circumstances impel officials to break faith with their employer and seek additional forbidden sources of income. Those are the salaries paid, the opportunities presented for illegal use of office and policing to mean both detection and punishment. Obviously, corruption will be most prevalent when salaries are low, opportunities great and policing weak. It will be infrequent when the reverse applies, and salaries are generous, opportunities few and policing strong. But, in case of Civil services personnel, it has never been alleged that salaries for this group were the law in the conventional sense of being insufficient to support a customary standard of living. It was rather that the opportunities with which they were presented suddenly proliferated. This first occurred during the second world war, when control were imposed on the economy.

To control the malady in 1945 the Delhi Special Police Establishment (DSPE) was set up with the special task of investigating and prosecuting corruption in the Central Government. In 1964 it WAS absorbed into a newly created Central Bureau of Investigation (CBI) as its investigative arm. This is the only body of police organisation remains in the Central government. All other police forces are State responsibilities. Despite best efforts given by the CBI, it has not been possible to discover an increasing number of corrupt officials for manifold reasons. Though corruption may have contained, it has not been, reduced. For this there seems to be two reasons. First, opportunities continue to abound. To take only a few instances, licences and permits are required for a great number of activities, contract have to be placed for defence and other supplies, the nationalised banks extend credit to cultivators', many of wham are illiterate and easily duped. These departments that deal most directly with the economy are also the most corrupt. The C.P.I. Report for 1980 gives detail of cases dealt with in the courts of 172 convictions fifty three (31 per cent) were officials from the Ministry of Finance (thirty six being from the public sector banks), twenty five (15 per cent) from the Railways, Twenty one (12 per cent) from the Ministry of Communications (mainly posts and telegraphs) and fourteen (eight per cent) from the Ministry of defence.

The second reason is weak policing. Prevention of corruption in the administration is primarily the responsibility of the departmental heads. But in practice they tend to see the fight against corruption as the task of the specialised agencies. Political corruption is one of the main reasons of weak policing on corrupt activities of the officials. When corrupt, the Ministers are unable to demand honesty in their civil servants with any degree of conviction. Very often they serve as a model and an excuse for the corrupt official. It has recorded regretfully that political corruption in India is increasing and involves even the very highest levels of government. One cannot therefore expect any policing effort to come from that quarter.

Corruption is a socio-economic offence and also called white colour crime. The white colour criminal is an avaricious criminal person. It is his greed that is the cause of his crime. Prevention and control of corruption has been and continue to remain as a burning issue in India as appears from the failure of efforts to combat it. We have had innumerable Commissions of inquiry on corruption. The Railway Corruption inquiry Committee under Acharya Kripalani (1953), The Vivian Bose Commission (1962), the Santhanam Committee on Prevention of Corruption (1964), the Wanchoo Committee Report on Black Money (1971). We have set up Special Police Establishment and Vigilance unite in departments of administration at the centre and similar units set up in States. We have Union Public Service Commission and State Public Service Commissions to see that people are selected on merit and not to favour friends or relatives. We have also laws to combat corruption. Time to time amendment of such laws also done to implement it more effectively. The Prevention of Corruption Act 1947 has been amended in 1988. But none of them have succeeded even to the slightest degree in reducing the general prevalence of corruption, nepotism, black marketing, adulteration of food and drink, adulteration of drug etc. The reasons are manifold and multiferous. A country where administration itself is corrupted cannot expect a corruption free public life. All the ideals of socialism and collective wealth which seem to inspire our law makers are subverted by the misuse of the enormous power and patronage placed in the hands of ministers and officials. On the official front, the forms of corruption are similar to that on the political front. The two parties have to reciprocate in order to earn money by illegal means, earn the favour of newsmen getting relatives and friends jobs they are actually not qualified for or promotion import quotas that sell in the black at steep premium and so on. The objective of the official of course is different from the politicians. Under the auspices of this system the guardians of law commit crimes, They and the underworld of crime find anti-social elements have mutually advantageous relations hold up men and protection of racketeers and regular stipends from brothels, gambling dens, narcotic pedlars and smugglers.

One of the Santhanam solutions against corruption was to reduce discretionary powers of different categories of government servants. Discretionary power is highest at bureaucratic level. Corrupt officials at this level misuse their discretionary power for personal gain causing injustice and deprivation. Companies and businessmen should be obliged to keep detailed accounts of the expenditure in their expense account. Normally it is the duty of the Income Tax officers to scrutinise these accounts. But, whenever an Income-Tax officer feels that amounts have been spent for entertaining high officials, or other purpose for which satisfactory explanation is not forthcoming, it should be his duty to refer the matter to the chief vigilance officer in the department concerned,

Great care should be exercised in selecting officers for appointment to high administrative posts. Only those whose integrity is above board should be appointed to these posts. During British regime, the Indian civil Service (I.C.S.) officers were working as key administrators in the government system. Although the I.C.S. ceased to function as a service of the Secretary of State for India after the 15th August, 1947 when the Indian Independence Act, 1947 was enforced, its members were automatically appointed to corresponding posts under the crown in connection with the affairs of the dominion of India or of a Province by virtue of the provisions of Sub-Clause (l) of Clause 7 of the Indian (Provisional Constitution) order, 1947. Similar to the I.C.S., Indian Administrative Service

(I.A.S) were created in the same pattern and condition of service in the independent India and thereby the old bureaucratic framework retained. I.A.S. officers are the key personalities forming the administrative machinery in the country. The State Civil service officers along with I.A.S. officers managing the administrations in States. Several forms of corruption appears at different levels. A bribe taken by a peon is called "bakshis" and a clerk "mamooli". It is reshwat or utkoch when accepted by a senior official. A Minister takes it in the name of party funds. Some clever officials raise frevolous objections or queries to deliberately delay matters. The senior officers who are corrupt and incapable to deal with matters of concerned administration are accentric in nature and try either to victimise or suppress the junior officers who are not submissive to their corrupt activities. Administrative delays are one of the major causes of corruption. Quite often delay is deliberately contrived so as to obtain some kind of illicit gratification.

Under the prevailing system of administration, the number of bureaucrats has increased enormously with the result that decisions are avoided, responsibility shrinks and papers are floated up and down the hierarchical ladder, thus delaying decisions and keeping people waiting for unduly long periods. The bureaucracy must be made accountable not only for its actions but also its inaction in view of the current tendency that safety and profit lie in doing nothing. Among all the corrupt public servants, bureaucrats are most advantageous group by way of acting as disciplinary authority. A bias administrator may make his defence against corruption more advantageously then his subordinates. So, it is necessary to have an inspection agency that would carry out rendom checks at all levels of the administration, to ensure quick disposal of cases and detect corruption and delay at all levels. Efficiency, honesty, merit and performance are to give more importance than to mere seniority for promotion at all levels specially at the higher echelons. Creation of laws against corruption as proved not at all effectives to deal with corruption. Under the prevailing circumstances the custodian of laws are the law breakers.

7

Conclusions

The present dissertation attempts to study and to investigate systematically the causes of proliferation of corruption, efficacy of its control in the modern Indian society with special reference to Assam. The ever increasing corruption syndroms has entered into the body politic of the modern society. Rampant corruption case with the increased economic activity and political apathy. The mounting pile of corruption creates increasing complexities of their control. Increase in complaints, investigation, prosecutions departmental proceedings and punishment entail more intensified tussle against corruption than any increase in it. Even though, a situation has developed in the modern Indian society where each individual's corruption is limited only by the limited scope he finds for it and it exists in a wide dimensions beginning from the top echelons down to the lowliest low in the society.

India has the longest history of anti-corruption work, prevalence of corruption never fails to evoke a gushing torrent of abuse, even from the most docile. This canker is fast destroying our economy and our morale. People now have come to believe that those in authority are themselves corrupt and so do not wish to improve matters though they make a lot of noise to distract attention from this and to meet the rising tide of criticism Corruption has spread in the society as an epidemic disease and haunting the conscience of the nation. People are now do not rely on the means of controlling corruption, yet in practice we must evolve our own method through trial and error to tackle this problem; depending on the nature and depth of its roots. Corruption amongst public servants is most prevalent when salaries are low, opportunities great for illegal use of office and policing weak. So, it is best to analyse the problem critically and expose inadequacies of the rule of law available for its control.

In order to effectively check corruption much remains to be done positively and constructively. The existing laws dealing with corruption must have some deficiencies causing failure to check corruption upto the desired extent. The findings of litigations in court cases under different provisions proves inadequacy of anti-corruption laws at least in some specific areas. Beginning with the provision of anti-corruption law regarding previous sanction necessary for prosecution, it is revealed from the judicial pronouncements in many cases, that the prosecution of most corrupt public servants may fail due to procedural wrangling resulting from exclusive executive lapses assessed under S. 161 or S. 164 or S. 166 of the I..P.C. (45 of 1860) or under Sub-section (2) (or Sub-section 3 A) of S. 5 of the P.C. Act, 1947 in respect of provisions of sanction. The famous Antulay litigation in Bombay High Court and many other litigations in the Supreme Court and High Courts in India Highlights the deficiencies in the existing provisions of granting previous sanction for prosecution. The common complaint is that at the top there stays presiding deities of corruption in ease and hence are not interested in tackling corruption. Coupled with this is the charge of double standards of ethics, which they claim are applied to the tenants of political summit and their do-gooders. The approach in the Antulay litigation was in accordance with the policy underlying S.6 is that a public servant is not to be exposed to harassment of a frivolous or speculative prosecution. It was held in R.S.

Nayak -V- A.R. Antulay that, where offences as set out in S. 6 are alleged to have been committed by a public servant, sanction of only that authority would be necessary who would be entitled to remove him from that office which is alleged to have been misused or abused or corrupt motives. Existence of a valid sanction is a prerequisite to the taking of cognizance of the offences. In the absence of such sanction, the court would have no jurisdiction to take cognisance of the offence.

In R. Menon -V- Union of India, 1966, LJ (c)387, where the accused ceased to be a public servant at the time the court took cognizance of offence, it was decided that the 3. 6 of the Act, does not apply.

In Dharmadatan, K.S. -V- Central Government, A.I.R. 1979; S.C. 1495 (2 Judges) (1973)2 SCJ, 391; 1979, Cr.L.J. 1127, it was held by the Supreme Court that S. 19 (old Sec. 6) applies only where at the time when the offence was committed, the offender was acting as a public servant. As the appellant had ceased to be a public servant at the time when the cognizance of the case was taken against him by the special Judge, no sanction under S. 19 (old Sec. 6) was necessary.

In Nirmalendu Biswas-V- State, it was held by the Gauhati High Court, that the sanction for High Court, prosecution of the appellant granted without authority and hence is a nullity.

Interpretation

It is evident from the decisions of the Supreme Court and High Courts in India in many cases of corruption and bribery, that the existing provision of S. 6 (now section 19) of the Prevention of Corruption Act, regarding previous sanction necessary for prosecution often leads to failure in penalising corrupt. If the accused has ceased to be a public servant at time when the court is called upon to take cognizance of the offence alleged to have been committed by him as public servant, S. 19 (old Sec. 6) is not attracted (R.S. Nayak -V- A.R Antulay). The Supreme Court observed that when the provisions of 6 (new Sec. 19) of the Act, are examined it is manifest that two conditions must be fulfilled before its provisions become applicable. First the offences mentioned therein must be committed by a public servant while discharging statutory duties, secondly the public servant is employed in connection with the affairs of the Union of India or a State and is not removable from his office save by or with the sanction of the Union Government or the state Government or is a public servant who is removable from his office by any other competent authority (S.A. Venkataraman -V- State). Both these conditions must be present to prevent a court from taking cognisance of an offence mentioned in the section without the previous sanction of the Union Government or the State Government or the authority competent to remove the public servant from his office. If either of these conditions is lacking the essential requirements of the section do not stand in the way of a court taking cognisance without a previous sanction.

In the Prevention of Corruption Act, 1988, the change in S. 6 (now section 19) has been made only in Sub-section (3) and (4) Now sanction cannot challenged in any court unless failure of justice has in fact occasioned and unless the objection, if possible has been raised at an earlier stage in the proceedings. Not only this, no proceedings can be stayed even unless in the opinion of the court any failure of justice has occasioned. Though the intention of the Legislature in providing for sanction under S. 19 (old section 6) is not to shield the guilty persons, there was scope for the delinquent to escape by raising the technical plea of invalidity of sanction.

Public Servant Taking Gratification

The provision of the Prevention of Corruption Act, 1947,

as amended from time to time are severe to put down bribery and corruption but they also aim at protecting public servants from victimisation and unnecessary harassment in being dragged into frivolous and vexatious proceedings. Under the provisions, the prosecution sanctioning authority has important function to discharge.

The main ingredients of the charge of an offence under Section 7 (old section 161 IPC) of the Act as observed by honourable Justice Ranganath Mishra in R.S. Nayak -V- A.R. Antulay are:

1. that the accused was a public servant.
2. that he must be shown to have obtained from any person any gratification other them legal remuneration and
3. that the gratification should be as a active or reward for doing or forbearing to do any official act or for showing or forebearing to show, in the exercise of his official function, favour or disfavor to my person,

The prosecution in this case failed due to absence of the ingredient No. 1.

In C.T. Eden -V- State of U.P the Supreme Court laid down that explanation to S. 7 of the Act (old S. 161 I.P.C.) provides that the word gratification is not restricted to pecuniary gratification or to gratification estimable in money. Therefore there is no justification for not giving the word at gratification' its meaning.

IN the case of State of Bihar - Baswan Singh, the Supreme Court has stated that corroboration need not be evidence that the accused committed the crime, it is sufficient even though it is merely circumstantials evidence of disconnection with the crime.

In Rao Shiv Bahadur Singh -V- State of Vidhya Pradesh, The supreme Court held that the evidence of the witnesses who were not willing parties to the giving of the bribe and were only actuated with the motive of trapping the accused could not be treated as the evidence of accomplices. But their evidence was nevertheless, the evidence of partisan witnesses who were out to trap the accused and could not be relied for implicating the accused without independent corroboration.

In Jai Narain -V- State, the appellant had admitted recovery of the amount from his pocket. His explanation was rejected on account of the infirmities. It was held by the Supreme Court that he was rightly convicted in the absence of the corroborative evidence.

Interpretation

It is noticeable from the findings of many litigations in court cases of bribery and corruption that it is very difficult to establish a case of taking gratification by a public servant, though the dimension of this serious type of crime is miserably wide in public life. The giving and taking of bribe, according to legal provisions is a crime and the relevant sections under the PC Act, provides for punishment of a public servant taking a bribe. But the section is applied only when it is established that the accused received gratification which was not legal remuneration as a motive or reward. The section does not provide for punishment of the giver of bribe. It is essential to provide punishment of both bribe giver and taker. As bribery and corruption starts from the top echelons and reaches the lowest ebb in the society, it is not possible to account, how many corrupt are there and how such they made in a given time. It becomes a regular feature of day to day life and a matter of speculation only. The corrupt are too many, their methods too devious and their accomplices too great in number. A very small proportion of the corrupt are caught in the legal net. Therefore laws are not adequate answer to the menace of corruption. S.7 of the P.C. Act, (old S. 161 of I.P.C.) provides punishment against the public servant who obtain gratification for doing or forbearing to do any official act or for allowing or fore bearing to show in the exercise of his official functions, favour or disfavour to any person or for rendering or attempting to render say service or disservice to any person with any authority. One of the important ingredients of the offence under the section is to detect whether the accused had received the gratification as a motive or reward, It is not easy to establish the presence of this ingredient. As such in majority cases the accused is acquitted. Secondly if the giver of gratification is not an interested witness, the detection becomes complicated.

However the change in law made by the 1988 amendment of the Act, by creating a new offence called "criminal misconduct" as defined in clauses (a), (b), (c) and (d) of S. 13 (1) (old S.5 (1)) makes the provisions more effective in trapping delinquents habitually accepting gratification and valuable things. The scope of the offence under S. 13 (1) (d) (old S.5 (l) (d)) of the Act is wider than that of the offence under S.7 to 9 (old S. 161 to 163 I.P.C.). Under S. 13 (2), a public servant can be punished on the charge of criminal misconduct irrespective of motive or reward for showing favour. Provisions for receiving awards by Government servants are also being made by a separate, but substantially similar sets of conduct Rules enacted by State legislature. At present, two sets of such rules are in force for Assam government services, "The Assam Services (Discipline and Appeal) Rules, 1964" and the Assam Civil Services (Conduct) Rules, 1965. The provisions however are not being strictly followed, and as a result in majority of prosecutions, the corrupt public servants escape from punishment. On the contrary, public servants who perform their duties impartially, without any fear or favour and strictly in accordance with law or rules fail to provide corrective justice due to highhandedness and political interference in favour of the corrupt public servant.

Inspite of creating scope by new amendments of the P.C. Act, the corruption in our country become a convention, a tradition, a psychological need and necessity. Such a regular practice cannot be eradicated from our society without a radical change in the environment. A High standard of ethical behaviour of the people right from top to bottom alongwith an effective change in the administrative structure is needed to fight corruption.

Many cases of corruption remains suppressed and undetected and the corrupts are being freed from any legal action due to administrative negligence of motive or inefficiency. Such cases are countless in number. Two such instances are cited below:

Case No. 1

Departmental proceeding against Sri A.Y. Ahmad district Agricultural officer, Aizal: Enquiry Report No Agri/ Hills /ADA-2/73-80/33 dt. 11.6.80.

This is a case of misappropriation detected in the year 1971. The summery of findings of enquiry on the departmental proceedings submitted by Sri G.C Sharma, Additional Director of Agriculture (Hills) was that -

1. the misappropriation of Govt. money by Sri Ahmed to the tune of Rs. 5,14,853.06 has been established and he now stands liable to this amount. Rule No. 11 under "Assam Contingency Manual" itself dictates the punishment for such refund of expenditure improperly incurred.
2. As charged it was not deriliction of duty, but proved to be a deliberate action for misappropriation.

3. the charge of serious misconduct on the part of the officer is also found to be correct.

Altogether nine charges were levelled in the enquiry report against Sri Ahmed. Sri Ahmed retired from service while the case of misappropriation was in the process for action for an indefinite period. In the meantime Sri Ahmed filed a case in the Session Court, Guwahati claiming his pensionary benefits under C/R No. 886 of 1987. Due to negligence on the part of the government to submit replay to the court for an indefinite period, an Ex-parte decree has been given in favour of the accused.

Case No. 2

A programe of supplying potato seeds to the flood affected cultivators was implemented in 1986 by the Assam Seeds Corporation Ltd. for an amount of Rs. 4.00 crores. On allegations being raised in the Assam Legislative Assembly by an opposition member regarding irregularities and misappropriation of this programme, the matter was discussed in the Assam Cabinet and forced an Inquiry Committee to find out the facts for punishment of officials responsible for the lapses.

The salient points of the inquiry report presented to the House on 18th March, 1988 were as follows.

The potato seeds were supplied by some traders obtaining license from the Directorate of Agriculture for an amount of Rs. 4.00 crores for distribution to cultivators. It was also alleged that the potato seeds were purchased from Fancy Bazar, Guwahati instead of supplying certified seeds and that too in higher prices.

In order to arrive at a decision on the issue quoted above, the Inquiry Committee decided to examine—

1. the privailing prices of table as well as seed potatoes in the States of Meghalaya, West Bengal, Bihar, U.P. and H.P.
2. Availability of seed potato in Assam and other States.
3. Whether the suppliers of the alleged seed potato were traders and if so their standing as seed dealers.
4. The procedures followed in inviting tenders.
5. Departmental investigation conducted on the alleged departmental irregularity.

During examination of various record, the Inquiry Committee noted that most of the tenderers obtained seed licenses from the Director of Agriculture after the advertisement issued by the M.D., Assam Seeds Corporation Ltd. on 10th Oct., 1986. In a number of cases, the tenders were considered without considering the first requirement viz. as dealers in the seed dealing business possessing the seed dealing license well before the time of advertisement. The Inquiry Committee further learnt that the A.S.C. considered three cases on the basis of a letter written by a Joint Director of Agriculture (Pulse) in violation of the terms of the advertisement. The Committee also came across overwriting, alteration in the tender papers. The Inquiry Committee therefore decided to obtain a written clarification from the M.D., A.S.C. on these points. On examination by the Inquiry Committee it was found that 17 tenders obtained dealing license after the issue of the notification/advertisement on 16th Oct. 1986 inviting tenders and three tenders obtained license after the closing date from the Director of Agriculture.

The Inquiry Committee after examination of various aspects recommended that a thorough probe should be made into the affairs of the potato seeds deal by an independent authority so as to enable the Government to proceed against the persons at fault and to streamline the administration of the Directorate of Agriculture and the Assam Seeds Corporation. Since then the case is under investigation and the corrupt public servants of this case are yet to be brought to the legal net for punishment.

Interpretation

It is revealed from the style of administration and functioning in the Government Department that little action is taken by the authorities in departments against the corrupt practices when such cases come to their notice Delay in departmental proceedings and initiation of necessary actions in each case in time causes hardship in conviction of delinquents.

Another important factor responsible for the escape of a good number of corrupt people is that the P.C. Act provides punishment to corrupt public servant only. As such those who cannot be accommodated with the definition of 'public servant' has no scope for prosecution, causing increase in corruption indiscriminantly. Corruption by persons other than public servants particularly those who are in power can practise in a rampant way without fear and consequences. The Antulay nexus between political power and money has existed since imperial ages in the history,

A meaningful socio-legal study of this important piece of legislation aimed at maintaining rectitude and integrity in political and public life. As suggested by the Law Commission of India in its 29th report (1966), change in law is required to ensure speedy trial of cases of bribery, corruption and criminal misconduct and make the law otherwise more effective.

Though there have been some well meaning, but ineffective attempts to check the evil including the recent amendments in the Prevention of Corruption Act, 1947, hiking of corruption in public life becomes increasingly complex and unchecked, instead of being saddled. The proliferation of corruption has resulted from manipulation of power. This power is manifested negatively, in the effective insulation of the corrupt appropriations of income and advantage from denunciation and removal.

Among all the forms of corruption so far identified, public servant talcing gratification other than legal remuneration in respect of an official act and taking gratification or obtaining valuable things for exercise of personal influence with public servant are seems rising in number. A corrupt officer himself may be efficient, but he fishes in the inefficient and slow processes of the Government, around him. Most of the corrupt inducements aimed not so much to alter administrative decisions in their favour, rather to expedite them. In most of the cases, the anxiety to avoid delay has encouraged the growth of dishonest practices like the system of speed money which has become a common type of practices particularly in matters relating to the award of contracts Two important factors (1) unwarranted secrecy in the transaction and (2) unbridled discretion vested in officials, offered scope for dishonest practice of ' speed money in the offices. For existence of corruption in public life two groups viz. one who are willing to corrupt and the other who are willing to be corrupted appear to co-exist peacefully. As such bribe givers are also not less responsible for the practices of corruption. But in the P.C. Act, there is no provision for punishing the bribe giver.

Among the attempts so far *made* by the Government to combat corruption, the setting up of the Santhanam Committee in 1962 to review existing instruments and to advice on practical measures to make anti-corruption measures more effective is a very important step. It was asked to consider and suggest steps to be taken to emphasise the responsibilities of each depart-meat for checking corruption. It was also to suggest changes in the Government servants conduct rules' ensure speedy trial of cases of bribery, corruption and criminal misconduct and such steps as the secure public support for the various anti-corruption measures in order to create a climate conducive to the improvement of public morals. Accordingly the Committee recommended lot of changes in the anti-corruption laws and other measures. But, it is a matter of great discontent that, the Government of India excluded from the Santhanam Committee investigation of corruption among Ministers. If there is corruption in the administration, the ministers are primarily and ultimately responsible for it. The corrupt Ministers definitely are not willing to take action against their corrupt colleagues and subordinates. If Ministers are above board, they can prevent corruption among the services. At present the code of conduct for Ministers, M.P.s and M.L.A.'s is of imperative necessity to deal with corruption in a realistic approach. Amendment of anti-corruption laws and other steps as per recommendation of the Santhanam Committee alone is not sufficient to deal with corruption effectively. Each and every corrupt people be brought to the legal net irrespective of their status and position.

With the increase of population and cost of living, things become more complicated and alongwith such complications, corruption is also mounting day by day. People become selfish and they are busy to manage individual interest rather than to think for the nation, to preserve morality or to think for others equally. Officials become more and more corrupt to improve their livelihood and to meet their materials need. Public in general willing to corrupt to move the file in his favour, to obtain contract, to obtain supply order, to obtain job, and whatever else. In most of the cases politicians are working as initiator of corruption. So far the preparation of the code of conduct for legislators and ministers was concerned the Central Government had responded by adopting a code of conduct for Ministers. But in State except a few nothing has yet been done in this regard which is very urgent if the corruption of the politicians and in turn corruption in public life is to be prevented. As per recommendation of the Administrative Reform Commission, 1966, two tier machinery of Lokpal and Lokayukts are to be instituted. In Assam, the Assam Lokayukta and Uplokayukta Act, 1985 has sanctioned and received the assent of the President of India on 12th December, 1986. The Act made provisions for appointment and functions of Lokayukta and Up-Lokayukta in Assam. Accordingly a Lokayukta has been appointed for Assam for the investigation of grievances and allegations against Ministers, Legislators and other public servants in certain cases and for matters connected therewith. If the Lokayukta is functioning as per objectives without fear and strict to the provisions, the rampant corruption practices of Ministers and Legislators in particular can be reduced, if not abolished. The above analysis leaves us in no doubt about our failure to equip ourselves with a high powered, impartial machinery to tackle corruption in high places. We should have a permanent machinery to probe into the present rot and to act a deterrent against future abuse of power by men in high position.

It is difficult to be precise about the dimensions of corruption. Yet the ugly facts and figures are formidable. Huge number of cases of complaints pending for disposal at all levels in different stages like vigilance establishments, special court, C.B.I special Police Establishments etc. Delay in deciding cases for discriminant period may cause ventilation of corruption. So, speedier decision of such cases are needed as a part of effective measures to combat corruption.

Coupled with importance of knowing the anatomy of corruption is the causes of the disease so that a correct diagnosis can equip us for devising both preventive and corrective measures. So our anti-corruption drives must be to prevent and rectify the primary causes of corruption such as - stark inefficiency, inordinate delay undeserved patronages, raw nepotism, donating to election funds, judicious regulation of public norms, abject poverty tax leadership, unhinged, controls black market speed money, cloistered security, worship of the filthy lucre, liasion between business houses and politicians, lack of popular vigilance, lack of willingness to tackle corruption, corruption amongst anti-corruption officials. The Santhanam Committee's suggestions for tightening disciplinary procedures against civil servants and plugging loopholes is the existing laws and anti-corruption drives are by and large very well thought out and expect good results if implemented faithfully. In the twenty nineth report of The Law Commission of India it was cemented that—if anti-corruption activities are to be successful, it must be recognised that it is as important to fight these unscrupulous agencies of corruption as to eliminate corruption in the public services. In fact they go together.

Law enforcement agencies without morality cannot yield objective results, since the fabric of civilised law might be blended with morality and justice. Morality amongst all groups of people including officials should be harmonised for a clean public life. On the basis of the prevailing situations and environment the following recommendations may be suggested for eradication of corruption in public life:

1. Harmonising morality amongst people of elite class.
2. Training people to be laborious for economic upliftment.
3. To have only the minimum needs of property irrespective of earning.
4. Appointment of efficient and honest personnel in Anti-Corruption departments.
5. Computerisation of informations and investigation system.

6. Stoppage of migration for minimising demands of needs and resources needs and resources.
7. Increasing administrative efficiency of Government machinery to render quick and effective services.
8. Prompt action against corrupt public servants.
9. Officers responsible for failing to take action or delaying action against delinquents should be suitably punished.

For such measures the amendment to relevant provisions in the existing statutes are to be completed on priority basis. The hydra-headed demon of corruption must not be allowed to stay a moment longer. The irrational resignation that corruption is the order of the day and has assumed international recognition must be uprooted. Both law and morality must be Dressed into service to do the needful to restore the glow and glory of clean and honest public life.

Public vigilance is the basis of any anti-corruption strategy. It lies with the public, which should be prepared to put up stiff fight against it. For every corrupt officials there are hundreds of members of the public wanting to take use of him. It will therefore be very difficult to tackle this growing evil unless we mobilise the best elements in society to fight it.

Bibliography

BOOKS

Chandra, M. (1979), *Socioeconomic Crime*, p. 60.

Chales, R. Swanson and Leonard Territo (1983), *Police Administration*, p. 23.

Coleman, J.W. (1987), *The Criminal Elite*, p. 155.

Deb, R. (1968), *Police and Law Enforcement*, p. 55.

Deb, R. (1988), *Police and* Law *Enforcement*, p. 166.

Deb R. (1988), *Principles of Criminology, Criminal Law and Investigation:* 2nd Ed., Vol. II, p. 395.

Deb, R. (1988), *Police and Law Enforcement*, p. 111.

Deb. R. (1978), Public services Under The Rule of Law Right to Disobey illegal Orders, *Journal of the Indian Law, Institute*, Oct. to Dec. 1978, p. 574.

Deb, R. (1980), Public Services Under the Rule of Law: *Indian Police Journal;* Ministry of House Affairs, Government of India; Jan. to March 1980, p. 43.

Deb, R. (1982), *Principles of Criminology, Criminal Law and Investigation.*

Indrayan, N.K (1985), *Law of Public Opinion in India*, p. 180.

Michael, C. (1983), *Corruption, Causes, Consequences and Control: Bureaucratic Corruption and Its Remedies*, p. 207.

Michael C. (1983), *Corruption, Causes, Consequences and Control*, p. 211.

Micheal, C (1983) Corruption, Causes, Consequences and Control: The Land of Waving palms political Economy Corruption Inquiries and Politics in Sierra Leone, p. 194.

Monterio, J.B. (1966) *Corruption*, p. 109.

Nemisharan, M. (1991), *World Famous Corrupt Politicians*, p. 26

Paranjape, N.V. (1983), *Criminology and Penology*, p. 78

Qadri, S.M.A. (1382), *Crime, Society and Law*.

Ranchhoddas and Thakore, D.K. (1978), *The Indian Penal Code;* 2nd Ed., 1978.

Ryley C. (1935), *Tan Thousand Public Economies*, Blue Ribbon Books.

Swaroop, V. (1990), *Prevention of Corruption*, Act, 1988, p. 396

REPORTS

Committee on Prevention of Corruption (1964), Santhanam Committee; p. 110.

Law Commission of India (1958), Fourteenth Report, Vol. II, p. 736, 742 (1958).

Law Commission of India (1966) Twenty Ninth Report, Feb. 1966.

Public Accounts Committee (1953), Audit Report, Assam.

Committee on Prevention of Corruption (1968) Ministry of Home Affairs, Govt. of India, New Delhi, Aug. 17, 1963.

Report of the Gaming Board for Great Britain (1976), H.C. 253, 1977, Para 46-7 and 1977, H.C. 278, 1977, para 26.

Report of the Committee on Prevention of Corruption (1963) Santhanam Committee, p. 46.

ARTICLES

Bhargava, G.S. (1989), "Political Corruption", *Mainstream,* Dec. 30, pp. 15-20.

Chittaranjan, C.N. (1982), "Corruption: who is to Fight it?" *Mainstream,* May, 1982

Chockalingam (1969), in re 1969, *Mad. I.W.* (Cr.) 90.

Govind, H. (1979), "Corruption, Causes end Cure," *Mainstream* (Republic day Issue).

Kant, K. (1962), "Corruption and Electoral Process", *Mainstream,* July 17, 1982.

Kanatkar, I.P.G.V. (1959). "Visit to Europe", *Bombay, Police Journal,* Vol. x, No 1, Jan. 1959, p. 4.

Limy, M. (1982), "How Grave is the Threat to the Nation," *Mainstream,* p. 21.

Sen, S. (1979), "Time to Fight Corruption," *Mainstream,* March 3, p. 23.

Shahabuddin, S. (1982), "Toning Up the Bureaucracy," *Mainstream,* Annual Issue, 1982.

Thesis, Monographs, Brochures, Papers etc.

Goswami, D.D. (1983), Administration of P.W.D. in Assam Since 1874 Ph.D. Thesis, p. 249.

High Denomination Bank Notes Act (1978) Demonetisation, 1978.

Sharma, Dr Sankar Dayal (1985) Sardar Vallabh Bhai Patel Memorial Lecture -II on Rule of Law and Role of Police, S.V.P. National Academy, Hyderabad, p. 14.

Index